The Open University

# Book 1 | Introducing environmental decision making

*by Chris Blackmore and Andrea Berardi
with the course team*

**T863 Environmental decision making: a systems approach**

This publication forms part of an Open University course T863 *Environmental decision making; a systems approach*. Details of this and other Open University courses can be obtained from the Student Registration and Enquiry Service, The Open University, PO Box 197, Milton Keynes, MK7 6BJ, United Kingdom: tel. +44 (0)870 333 4340; email general-enquiries@open.ac.uk

Alternatively, you may visit the Open University website at http://www.open.ac.uk where you can learn more about the wide range of courses and packs offered at all levels by The Open University.

To purchase a selection of Open University course materials visit http://www.ouw.co.uk, or contact Open University Worldwide, Michael Young Building, Walton Hall, Milton Keynes MK7 6AA, United Kingdom for a brochure: tel. +44 (0)1908 858785; fax +44 (0)1908 858787; email ouwenq@open.ac.uk

The Open University
Walton Hall, Milton Keynes
MK7 6AA

First published 2006.

Copyright © 2006 The Open University

All rights reserved. No part of this publication may be reproduced, stored in a retrieval system, transmitted or utilised in any form or by any means, electronic, mechanical, photocopying, recording or otherwise, without written permission from the publisher or a licence from the Copyright Licensing Agency Ltd. Details of such licences (for reprographic reproduction) may be obtained from the Copyright Licensing Agency Ltd of 90 Tottenham Court Road, London W1T 4LP.

Open University course materials may also be made available in electronic formats for use by students of the University. All rights, including copyright and related rights and database rights, in electronic course materials and their contents are owned by or licensed to The Open University, or otherwise used by The Open University as permitted by applicable law.

In using electronic course materials and their contents you agree that your use will be solely for the purposes of following an Open University course of study or otherwise as licensed by The Open University or its assigns.

Except as permitted above you undertake not to copy, store in any medium (including electronic storage or use in a website), distribute, transmit or retransmit, broadcast, modify or show in public such electronic materials in whole or in part without the prior written consent of The Open University or in accordance with the Copyright, Designs and Patents Act 1988.

Edited and designed by The Open University.

Typeset by The Open University.

Printed and bound in the United Kingdom by The Alden Group, Oxford.

ISBN N978 07492 02644

1.1

# Contents

Aims 5

## Part One 6

### 1 Introduction to decision making 6
1.1 What do we mean by decision making? 6
1.2 Approaches to decision making 6
1.3 Factors that influence decisions 10
1.4 Decision making and policy making 14

### 2 What do we mean by environmental decision making? 15
2.1 Concepts of environment 15
2.2 Environment and system 20
2.3 Characterising environmental decisions 22
2.4 Environmental decision making in the context of sustainable development 26
2.5 Sustainable development 26

### 3 Values, power and evolving discourse in environmental decision making 36
3.1 The importance of values 36
3.2 Power relations and sources within decision making 38
3.3 Evolving discourses concerning environmental decision making and sustainable development 41

### 4 Your experience of decision making and environmental decision making 45
4.1 Becoming aware of your actual and potential environmental decision making 45
4.2 Different levels of decision making 46
4.3 Recognising change and learning in decision situations 48

## Part Two 50

### 5 'Freedom to fly?' A case study in aviation expansion 50
5.1 Introduction 50
5.2 The need for an Aviation White Paper 52
5.3 The process leading up to the publication of the UK December 2003 Aviation White Paper 56
5.4 The December 2003 Aviation White Paper 76
5.5 Reaction to the Aviation White Paper 78
5.6 The future 80

| | |
|---|---:|
| Part Three | 84 |
| 6  The T863 framework for environmental decision making | 84 |
|     6.1  Environmental decision making as a learning process | 84 |
|     6.2  The T863 framework and the case study | 85 |
| Learning outcomes | 88 |
| References | 89 |
| Responses to Activities | 93 |
| Answers to Self-Assessment Questions | 105 |
| Acknowledgements | 108 |

Chris Blackmore wrote Part 1, and Andrea Berardi wrote Part 2. Part 3 was developed collaboratively by the T863 Course Team.

# Aims

In Book 1 we aim to:

- introduce the concept of environmental decision making
- introduce a range of concepts and discourses that are relevant to the context of environmental decision making
- introduce the concept of a system, its boundary and environment
- introduce some diagramming techniques that will enable you to start to explore these concepts and discourses
- encourage you, through activities, to begin to locate yourself within the context of environmental decision making
- provide a case study in environmental decision making as a starting point for your studies
- introduce an overarching framework for environmental decision making that will be considered in more depth in the following books.

## Study note

The suggested study time for this book is three weeks. In this time, you will need to engage with the material in this book and its associated readings and DVD elements, complete all the activities and self-assessment questions and complete your first tutor marked assignment (TMA). Further details of the TMA, including date and process for submission, are included in the assignment book. We advise that you spend one week studying Part 1, one week on Part 2 (the case study) and the third week on Part 3 and your TMA.

# Part One

# 1 Introduction to decision making

## 1.1 What do we mean by decision making?

We all make decisions in everyday life, both as individuals and in groups. These range from simple – for example, choosing what to eat, which route to take to work, which products to buy in the shop – to complex decisions about changing jobs, moving house, choosing schools and participating as a member of a local community in planning decisions and improvements.

What processes do we go through in making these decisions about different possible courses of action? Are they the same every time? Are they the same for everyone?

Just as there are different types of decision, there are also different approaches to decision making that are relevant in different circumstances.

Some decisions are made rationally and logically, while others are made more instinctively or less consciously, sometimes based on the smooth performance of a practised skill. Yet others appear not to be made intentionally at all, but are dictated by sudden changes in knowledge or circumstances – for example, when trying to decide between one route and another and finding that one way is blocked. In practice, other options may still be available but it appears as though the decision has been made for you. Variation in choice may also mean that one person has a decision to make and another does not. (My examples, above, of choosing what to eat or buy assume that I have a choice.)

Individuals and groups also have different preferences for how they make decisions and articulate what they do. Decision making is, at times, such a dynamic process that it can be difficult to tell whether a decision is being made or not. Whether we are directly involved in decision making (and in what capacity) or how we are affected by decisions others appear to have made, also affects our perspectives on decision making. So rather than give further examples here from my own perspective, I will now introduce some different approaches to decision making and ask you to draw on your own experiences.

## 1.2 Approaches to decision making

Think about some of the decision-making processes in which you have been involved. Do you recognise any of the following four approaches to decision making?

### (i) Rational choice

There are many variations on this theme. The aim is to identify and choose the best option in a particular set of circumstances by systematically going through a series of steps such as:

1. Consider the situation as a whole.
2. Identify the decision(s) that need(s) to be made.
3. Collect data on the range of alternatives.
4. Develop criteria for assessment of the alternatives.
5. Assess the alternatives against the criteria.
6. Choose one alternative.
7. Monitor the outcome of the decision.

In practice, you will rarely be making a decision in a static situation and may need several iterations of this type of process before you reach a decision. This is mainly because new alternatives or criteria emerge at a later stage. One example might be in deciding which computer to purchase to serve a group of people. Sudden availability of a cheaper or more powerful alternative, or changes in the composition of the group it has to serve, are examples of the sorts of change that can occur that will affect the outcome of the decision.

### (ii) 'Rational up-to-a-point' decision making

In situations where there is more uncertainty and limited data available it might only be possible or desirable to approach certain stages of the decision-making process rationally. Say, for example, you are allocating some small grants for local community improvements. You assess the proposals systematically and still end up with six very worthy projects from which you can choose only one. Some people would claim that you could continue to apply rational choice by going through further iterations of developing criteria and collecting data, but there will probably be diminishing returns from the additional effort. Another approach would be to select one of the final six quite randomly. Any of them would satisfice\* (represent an adequate or 'good enough' decision), at least from the perspective of those disbursing the grants.

### (iii) Decision making in disorder – the 'garbage-can' decision process

James March has written several critiques of ideas on rationality in decision making. The following quote and the idea of 'garbage-can decision making' comes from his 1982 article 'Theories of choice and making decisions'.

> Theories of choice underestimate the confusion and complexity surrounding actual decision making. Many things are happening at once; technologies are changing and poorly understood; alliances, preferences and perceptions are changing; problems, solutions, opportunities, ideas, people and outcomes are mixed together in a way that makes interpretation uncertain and their connections unclear.
>
> (March, 1982, p. 168)

\* The term *satisfice* describes a course of action that satisfies the minimum requirements to meet a goal rather than trying to achieve the maximum (biggest) or optimal (best) outcome. It was first coined by a key contributor to decision-making literature, Herbert A. Simon, in his *Models of Man* 1957.

The garbage-can metaphor describes the messy, complex and disordered way in which, at a particular moment in time, all decision makers are simultaneously involved in a range of activities and not just in a single decision-making process. These concurrent activities are all thrown together in the minds of decision makers, like in the jumble of a garbage can. March suggests that in such messy situations particular 'problems' and 'solutions' often become attached to each other because of their spatial and/or temporal proximity to each other, not because of rational choice.

This implies that understanding why decisions are made in one area frequently requires an understanding of what is going on elsewhere at the same time. The original work of March and his colleagues was done in the context of some university organisations. They described a situation where:

> Recent studies of universities, a familiar form of organized hierarchy, suggest that organisations can be viewed for some purposes as collections of choices looking for problems, issues and feelings looking for decision situations in which they might be aired, solutions looking for issues to which they might be an answer, and decision makers looking for work.
>
> (Cohen et al., 1972, p. 1)

It is not difficult to identify similar contexts today, with an environmental dimension, though not necessarily at the level of a single organisation, for instance when considering our use of technology in the context of climate change.

### (iv)  Personal beliefs approaches to decision making

There are many other personal theories and beliefs around decision making, based on an individual's experiences of decisions. Here are just a few:

'... toss a coin to make the decision, if you then want to make it the best of three you know which decision you want to make'

'... always dismiss the first and choose the next option that is better'

'... better to make any decision than no decision at all'

'... you never need to actually make any decisions if you just keep on endlessly collecting views and feeding them back to people until the decision is made'

'... you can tell whether it's the "right" decision by how you feel about it'.

### Study note

From reading the course guide you will be aware that two techniques are used in this course to help you read the text actively and critically: 'Activities' and 'Self-Assessment Questions' (SAQs). Activities will require you to either apply ideas or techniques from the text to your own situation, or to take stock of your own experiences and ideas before engaging with those described by others. Hence the responses to activities are your own and you may find it useful to record them in your learning journal or blog, so you can easily refer back to them later in the course. Author's responses to these activities are nearly always included at the end of the book just by way of illustration. SAQs, on the other hand, will usually be restricted to summarising points made in the text and testing whether you have fully understood the preceding material. Answers to all SAQs are provided and they are also at the end of the book.

## Activity 1  Consider your own decision-making experience

Consider your own experience of making decisions, or perhaps in actively refraining from making decisions. Note down examples where the (a) rational, (b) rational up-to-a-point, (c) garbage-can and (d) personal beliefs approaches to decision making seemed to apply (one for each). (My own response to this activity is included at the end of this book.)

In practice, most decision making involves a combination of approaches. So, why are people not completely rational in their decision making? James March in another paper, 'Limited rationality' (1994), claims that although decision makers try to be rational, in a particular context, they are constrained by limited cognitive capabilities and incomplete information, so although they often intend to be rational, their actions are often less than rational. Not being entirely rational is just part of being human! In this paper, March does not discuss the role of emotions in affecting rationality in decision making but he has written on this topic elsewhere (March 1978). There is a lot of literature on emotion and decision making related to understanding human cognition (the mental process of knowing and developing knowledge) and what motivates human behaviour, particularly in the areas of medical decision making and psychology (e.g. Schwarz (2000) and Ubel (2005)).

### Study note

My 'rational up-to-a-point' decision making is only a part of the 'limited rationality' ideas described by March. Elements of rationality appear at different stages. In practice, all but the rational choice option described in this section could be thought of in terms of limited rationality.

### Reading 1

Read the extract from March (1994), which you will find in Book 1 Readings and then answer the following SAQ on it.

## SAQ 1  Information constraints

What are the four main information constraints that March believes face decision makers in organisations? In your experience, are these constraints also relevant in non-organisational settings? (Note your answer in your journal or blog.)

## 1.3 Factors that influence decisions

Now that these different approaches to decision making have been considered it is possible to extract a number of linked factors that influence decisions:

1. The decision makers
2. The decision situation
3. Thinking in terms of a problem or an opportunity
4. Decision criteria
5. Time
6. People affected by the decision
7. Decision support – theories, tools and techniques

I will briefly consider each of these factors in turn. They will all come up again and be discussed in more detail later in the course.

### 1 The decision makers

Different people approach decision making in different ways. Individuals are unique in terms of their personalities, abilities, beliefs and values. They also each have traditions of understanding out of which they think and act. Even when the same data are apparently available to all, people will interpret and assimilate the data in different ways and at different speeds. Some people are very confident about weighing up a situation and making decisions, others less so. Some like to take more risks than others. Competences, such as the ability to listen to other people, also vary. Social pressures affect everyone to varying degrees and the approval or disapproval of friends and colleagues may be more important to the decision maker than being 'right' every time. Political beliefs also vary and people will rank differently, for example, individual and social gains from a situation.

Each individual develops personal beliefs and values, including those relating to their environment, through different life experiences, and hence brings a different perspective to a decision situation. Some people will also have more at stake in a decision outcome than others. There are therefore many issues around who is involved in decision-making processes and how they participate.

### 2 The decision situation

The garbage-can approach to decision making showed that the decision situation is often messy and complex and that apparently unrelated events can affect decision outcomes, depending on what else is going on at the time the decision is taken. For any individual or group there will be both 'knowns' and 'unknowns' in a decision situation. In the examples so far, in the text and in my response for Activity 1, the unknowns range from prices and models of computers to weather conditions and availability of people. It is not always easy to work out which aspects of a decision situation are relevant.

Elements of change, risk and uncertainty are common in decision situations and recognising and making sense of these elements are two of the main challenges that decision makers face. Risk implies that we know what the possible outcomes of a decision may be and that we know, or can work out, the probability of each outcome.

Uncertainty, on the other hand, implies that there are unknowns and that we can at best guess at possible outcomes and their probabilities or consider a range of imagined scenarios. There are ways of reducing some of these unknowns by using relevant data, techniques (for example, 'what if' modelling) and the experience of participants. Many of the ideas and techniques outlined in this course are intended to help you recognise and evaluate different aspects of decision situations, to work out which are relevant and what you can do about them.

## 3  Thinking in terms of a problem or an opportunity

When you have started to consider an issue and are approaching a decision, do you think in terms of opportunities, problems or both?

A potential problem can often be turned around by thinking about it differently.

For example, Shields Environmental in the UK have developed a business that provides two specialist services – reuse/recycling of mobile phones and reuse/recycling of telecommunications network equipment. Fonebak was one scheme they have developed. It was the world's first mobile phone recycling scheme to comply with all legislation. Over 18 million phones each year were being replaced in the UK around 2000 and without opportunities for reuse and recycling would have probably gone as potentially hazardous waste to landfill. In Fonebak's first two years of operation (2002–04) the company processed 3.5 million mobile phones for reuse and recycling, from 10,000 collection points across Europe. Many phones were reused to provide affordable communication in developing countries and those that could not be reused were recycled, with their materials put back into productive use. In taking up this opportunity Shields Environmental have not only developed a successful business but also enabled others to comply with environmental regulations.

Robert Chambers, in his book *Challenging the Professions* (1993), argues that there are two main disadvantages to thinking of a situation as a problem rather than as an opportunity. First, it has negative connotations, and secondly it can lead to misallocation of resources if we think in terms of problem solving rather than seeking out new opportunities. Problems and opportunities seem to me to have other characteristics also, which I have listed in Table 1. Do you agree with them? Can you think of any others?

Table 1  Comparison of characteristics of problems and opportunities

| Problem | Opportunity |
|---|---|
| Negative connotation | Implies positive action |
| Often used with adjectives like 'worrying' or 'difficult' | Often used with adjectives like 'exciting' or 'new' |
| Needs solving? | Implies choice |
| Can confine both thinking and action | Can liberate enthusiasm for dealing with a situation |
| Recognises constraints | Recognises new directions |
| A situation of disadvantage | Turning situation to own advantage |

I am not trying to suggest that all problems can be turned into opportunities. One person's problem may well be another's opportunity, which will not always help the person with the problem! But it is worth remembering that how a decision-making situation is thought of can affect what actions are taken, and that there might well be opportunities in what appears to be a problem situation.

## 4  Decision criteria

The criteria that are established and used to evaluate alternative courses of action in decision making will certainly affect the outcome of a decision. Different criteria will be appropriate in different situations but are often needed both to help make a decision and to make apparent the basis on which it is made.

In group decision making, exploring and deciding on criteria is one way of developing a shared understanding of a situation. Different decision makers with different beliefs and values are likely to identify different criteria and give a different weighting to them (see Figure 1). For example, finding an option for a new housing site that will satisfy (a 'good' decision) or at least satisfice (an 'adequate' or 'good-enough' decision) all those involved will usually mean compromises or trade-offs. Specific criteria can help to identify areas where there is agreement and disagreement. Criteria for the new housing site might include, for example, how existing land use is valued and by whom, services and housing provision available in the vicinity, likely disturbance or enhancement of the area and implications for road safety. There will be different views on what is acceptable for each of these aspects and often a need for negotiation. Criteria such as these are frequently worked out at different levels, as part of the regional as well as more local planning processes. Issues of participation in these different levels of decision making are discussed later, in both Books 2 and 3.

"That makes four 'Yes'es and one 'No, no, a thousand times no.'"

Figure 1   Source: *The New Yorker Magazine*.

## 5  Time

A decision is made at a particular time in a particular set of circumstances. The decision situation can change very rapidly so what appeared to be a rational decision at one time might later appear to be anything but that.

One aspect of the time dimension that is particularly apparent in the 'garbage-can' decision-making approach is that the outcome of a decision may be affected by concurrent, but otherwise only marginally related, events. One example of this might be the unexpected availability of additional resources or a reduction in resources because of another project going on at the same time elsewhere. Another example might be the way that strong opposition to, or support for, a new development may unexpectedly surface because of events elsewhere.

Time is also a factor that can affect the nature of people's participation in decision making. Skills are needed to be able to judge the urgency of decision-making processes, who needs to be involved in which stages of decision making within a particular time and resource frame and to what extent timing can be negotiated and with whom. Examples of how time factors can affect decision outcomes will be given later in the course, for instance in the aviation expansion case study later in this book.

## 6 People affected by the decision

People who are likely to be affected by a decision can have considerable direct or indirect influence on the outcome of a decision. There are many ways in which this can happen. People affected might be 'shareholders' or 'stakeholders'. Shareholders' interests are economic; stakeholders' interests in the decision are much broader than economic. Stakeholdings may be direct or indirect and will be discussed further in Book 2. Ways in which people affected can influence the decision range considerably. They may participate actively or proactively from the start, for example by being involved in the design of decision-making processes or in deciding on policy, or at other stages, e.g. through campaigning to try to overturn specific planning decisions, such as road building, industrial or housing development, or participate passively by withdrawing cooperation after the decision has been reached, such as refusing to use a facility that has been provided. There are issues of power to take into account in considering the nature of the influence that people affected by a decision can have. Some of these issues will be explored in Section 3.2.

## 7 Decision support – theories, tools and techniques

Many theories, tools and techniques have been developed to support and explain decision making, for example in medical, legal and organisational contexts. They may offer support to decision-making processes, depending on how they are used. For instance, the ability to model aspects of a situation may address some of the information constraints mentioned in Reading 1. But note also that March (1991) commented that 'any technology is an instrument of power that favors those who are competent at it at the expense of those who are not'. Power relations, the role of different stakeholders and expertise in decision making and use of models for decision support will be discussed later in this course. A great deal of literature also exists on areas such as decision theory and behavioural research on how decisions are made. As this course has a practical rather than theoretical bias the Course Team will not attempt a comprehensive review of this literature. We shall, however, include in the books some extracts from texts that we think are useful to support both thinking and action for environmental decision making. Details of techniques for decision making are also included in the *Techniques* book.

## 1.4 Decision making and policy making

Decision making is such an integral part of most people's everyday lives that it is sometimes difficult to tell where decision making starts and ends. In this course you will consider boundaries of decision-making processes at different levels in some detail, building on your own experience and using a detailed case study and many examples.

An activity closely allied to decision making, yet different, is policy making. Policies are plans, courses of action or procedures that are intended to influence decisions. As such, they form part of the context for decision making, often providing guiding principles. But decision making is also a part of policy making and there is a dynamic relationship between decision making and policy making. These two activities differ mainly in their purposes. A decision will usually be specific to a situation, even though it will be linked to other decisions in other situations. A policy however may apply more generically. Why does this difference matter? It matters when a decision made in one situation sets a precedent that may become a 'de facto' policy. Examples where this has happened can be found in planning processes where precedents set are taken into account when appeals are made regarding granting planning permission. De facto policy also applies in some countries regarding prosecution of small scale polluters, where it is not practical to implement environmental legislation in a literal sense in all cases. Developing policy for dealing with diffuse pollution (i.e. from multiple sources) within water catchments is an example where decision making interacts with policy making. Problems of diffuse pollution are widespread, and where practical ways of improving diffuse pollution situations have been found, these have influenced policy options. Evidence of how insights from practice have influenced policy in this area can be found in the work of some of the UK Rivers Trusts. (See the websites of the UK Association of Rivers Trusts (2006) and its members for further details.)

# 2 What do we mean by environmental decision making?

## 2.1 Concepts of environment

### Activity 2  Your understanding of environment

The term 'environment' is used in many different ways and in many different contexts. Before I go on to explain what I mean by it in the context of this course, take a few minutes to write down two or three sentences that describe your own understanding of it. (There is no author response for this activity because it is explained in the following text.)

The way in which our environment is perceived is central to the way in which we approach environmental decision making, so the concept of environment will be explored iteratively in this course. At this stage, I simply want to introduce the concept, to encourage you to be critical of how the term is used and to explain the way the term will be used.

The words 'environment' and 'environmental' appear a lot in everyday language. For instance I picked out reference to the environment, learning environments, the business environment, my home environment and environmental schemes in a couple of magazines I was reading recently. But in going on to read the articles in which those words appeared it became clear that those terms had little in common beyond a generic meaning of 'contexts' or 'surroundings'.

### Activity 3  Substituting words

Read the following paragraphs. Write down some other words that you think could be substituted for the words 'environment' or 'environmental'. Comment on how easy or difficult you found it to do this exercise and why. (You may also find it useful to compare your response with mine, which is given at the end of this book.)

(a) Concerns that the *environment* is being down-graded in EU policy-making have been fuelled by reports that major initiatives from the European Commission are to be delayed, and potentially watered down.

ENDS Report 366 (July 2005)

(b) The Court of Appeal has recently been required to consider the compatibility of the *Environmental* Assessment Directive with the UK system for dealing with outline planning applications.

Macrory (2005)

(c) Lack of Public Sector Transparency Distorts the Business *Environment*.

The Development Gateway Business Environment web page (2005)

(d) Hydro-electric power is pollution free and safe once it's up and running, although in creating it there can be tremendous disruption and upset to the *environment*, animals and nearby residents.

BBC Weather Renewable Energy – Water web page (2005)

(e) It brings together games players, makers, thinkers and artists in a unique *environment* where games fans and novices alike can experience a mix of old and new, fun and discussion in the context of cinema and media.

BBC website advertising the event 'Screenplay 2004'

---

David Cooper (1992) contrasted a distended notion of environment, where each person's environmental concern is supposed to extend everywhere 'from street corner to stratosphere', with the idea of a 'milieu' in which a person belongs and which they make their own. Their environmental concerns will begin 'at home' with their environments and the networks of meanings with which they are daily engaged.

### Activity 4  Which issues are yours?

Which environmental issues are yours? Look at the list below. It is extracted from the BBC News website (in 2005). I searched for 'environmental' and a long series of headlines appeared including those below. You could generate a similar list yourself. Notice, in my list, or your own, the wide range of issues that are considered to have an environmental aspect.

Which of the issues mentioned in the news headlines below seem distant or close to you? Which issues interest or concern you? (If none of these do, then try regenerating your own list to widen your selection.) Select three examples and note why they are of interest or concern to you. (Keep a copy of your response in your journal as it may be useful to you later on in the course.)

New-look [greenest] road on award shortlist

Fury as greenfield homes approved

Call for changes to housing plan

Sewage study creates red (River) Clyde

Campaigners fight nuclear reactor

Environment award for youngsters

Gold mine sparks battle in Peru

Timber scheme wins national award

Formal warning for cement works

Anti-social behaviour inherited

What really goes into a nappy?

Protests as furnace plan unveiled

General Electric doubles spend on green agenda

Azerbaijan's post-industrial hangover

Pollutant affects sex chromosome

Climate change message for city

Greenpeace opposes wind farm plan

Biodiversity project gets funding

Online campaign seeks fishing ban

Protestors arrested at G8 summit

River Jordan nearly running dry

Eco-Islam hits Zanzibar fishermen

In doing these two activities you will have encountered some different ideas about what constitutes 'environment' and 'environmental' and thought a little about what the terms mean to you and what aspects interest or concern you. But how will these terms be used throughout this course?

The environment of an entity can usually be described as that which surrounds it, affects it and in most cases is affected by it. The entity concerned may refer to an individual (as in my environment) or a group of living and/or non-living things (as in an organisation's environment). Used in its narrow and 'natural' sense 'the environment' often refers to our biophysical surroundings. But humans are part of nature. People are in continuous interaction with their environment as they depend directly or indirectly on it for food, water, air and shelter for their very existence. It is our life-support system and at times its physical elements will be part of us. As well as sharing our environment with other people, we share it with other living things (both animals and plants) on which we depend. However, the relationship between people and their environment has many dimensions – physical, biological, social, psychological, emotional, economic, even temporal – in terms of how we are currently affected by past decisions and how our decisions will affect us and other generations in the future. This course will generally use 'environment' in this broad sense acknowledging its many dimensions.

One useful way of representing the relationships between entities and their environment is to use a diagram, in this next case, a systems map. (See *Techniques* book Diagramming: Systems maps and/or DVD.) You will hear more about 'systems' and practice using these maps later, but for now Figure 2 uses systems maps to represent some different interpretations of the word environment and to experiment with boundaries. It is deliberately in draft form as it is trying to capture and represent a series of ideas about the concept of environment, from different perspectives, rather than showing a situation at a particular moment in time or a single system of interest, which would have a clear whole system boundary.

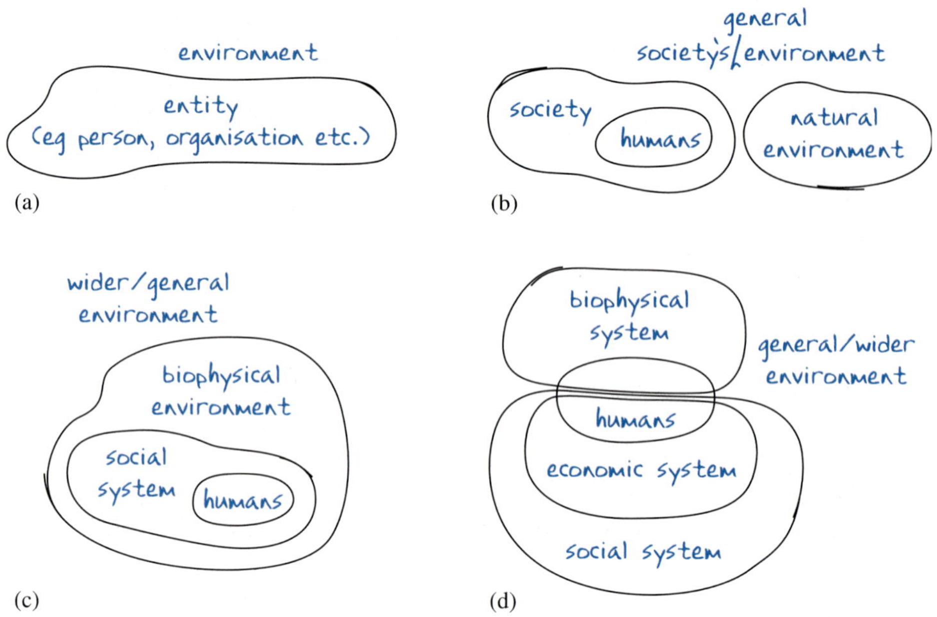

Figure 2  A series of draft systems maps, showing different relationships inherent in different definitions of environment (a) The general idea of environment as whatever surrounds something (b) Humans as part of society, which has a natural system in its general environment (c) Humans as part of a social system, operating within a general biophysical environment (d) Humans as part of social, economic and biophysical systems, within a general environment

There is much criticism of anthropocentric (human-centred) definitions of 'the environment' because they emphasise its utility value to people rather than recognising it has value in its own right (i.e. intrinsic or inherent value). These definitions also fail to recognise the way in which people are always in their environment not able to be separated from it. Human-centred definitions are also often thought to imply control by humans of physical and biological processes that we cannot control. They also fail to acknowledge the many feedback loops in our relationship with our environment. However, humans exist in societies, most of which use technology, and we certainly have the ability to affect some natural processes in our use of that technology, depending on how we choose to use it. For example, temperature, rainfall, sea levels and the composition of the atmosphere have all been affected by people's activities, such as burning fossil fuels for energy and transport or changing land use. Our use of 'green' technology, e.g. for renewable energy, might have less effect on natural processes, depending on how it is used (Figure 3).

Figure 3    People's activities affect natural processes

There are many possible choices about how we live and these choices are not simple to make, not least because the organisation of human societies is experienced by many as complex. Humans also affect and are affected by their environments just by living – breathing, eating, drinking, producing wastes, etc. – not only in their use of technology. In order to understand better the effects of our decisions and actions and how we might make necessary changes there is therefore a need to focus on what surrounds and affects humans, as well as their relationships with their environments. But it is important to keep in mind that there are many definitions of 'the environment' and to recognise that there are limits to what humans control (Figure 4).

Figure 4 'There are limits to what humans control' (a) Sicily's Mount Etna erupting in 2002 (b) A satellite image of Hurricane Katrina taken on 29 August 2005 as it passed through the USA Gulf Coast

## 2.2 Environment and system

We have already used the word 'system' in this book several times. The word system is used extensively in our 21st century vocabulary. For instance we refer to 'the transport system' or 'a home entertainment system' in a general way, not being specific about what we mean by system. Figure 2 in Section 2.1 used draft systems maps to explore some of the relationships in different definitions of 'environment'. It shows 'systems', their sub-systems and their boundaries with the system's environments. In experimenting with these diagrams we used the term 'system' in a different way from the general sense, to think in terms of systems. You will learn more about thinking in terms of systems and the importance of doing so in environmental decision making later in the course, particularly in Book 2. For now, you should note that it was possible to focus on some different systems, boundaries and environments in the different definitions, even though they started with the same word. Consider these further examples of systems from Sir Geoffrey Vickers, who was thinking of a school as a system:

> A school is a physical system which even small children can represent by a map. Its buildings are spatially related to each other. It has an apparent perimeter, but this dissolves on examination. For it is intersected by sewers, water mains, power lines, roads, each of which makes it part of some other system. To the school these are its physical support sub-systems. But to those who manage these supporting systems, the school is a component, making demands but also subject to demands, such as for example the demand to economize water in a drought. It may not readily occur to a child or even a teacher that for other professionals as estimable as they the school may properly be regarded as a generator of sewage. ... A school is far more than a physical system, supported by other physical systems. It is also an educational system, a social system, a financial system, an administrative system, a cultural system, all with an historical dimension.
>
> (Vickers, 1980, p. 5)

A system is not a fixed entity but the boundaries are identified by the observer and linked to purpose. Using the idea of a system raises some challenges for our use of the term 'environment'. Identifying the school's environment, if thinking of a school as a system, becomes a specific exercise of judging what lies within the system and what lies in its environment and the boundary between the two will vary with the observer's perceptions and articulation of the system's purpose.

Systems concepts and techniques have been found useful by many for identifying what is relevant in a particular situation and what may be changed. They are an essential part of this course and using the concept of system/boundary and environment is at its core.

In general terms there are some simple principles implicit in the idea of a system, as used by the T863 course team:

- A system is an assembly of components connected together in an organised way.
- The components are affected by being in the system and are changed if they leave it.
- The assembly of components does something.
- The system has been identified by someone as being of interest.

You may have come across systems ideas before, perhaps in other Open University courses, but most people learning about them for the first time find them easier to understand through examples of what they mean in practice. So what is meant by 'a systems approach' will be introduced in Book 2, by which stage you will be familiar with 'Freedom to fly?', the aviation expansion case study in Part Two from which examples will be drawn.

## 2.3 Characterising environmental decisions

Ken Sexton and his colleagues wrote a book called *Better Environmental Decisions – Strategies for Governments, Businesses and Communities* (Sexton et al., 1999) in which they characterise environmental decisions (see Table 2). They had a particular purpose in mind in doing this:

> Although the list is not exhaustive, it offers insight into the formidable task of categorising and evaluating different types of environmental decisions.

(Sexton et al., 1999, p. 5)

They structured their table around six dimensions:

1. At what social level does the environmental decision occur?
2. What are the important substantive aspects of the environmental decision?
3. What is the social setting for the environmental decision?
4. What is the mode of environmental decision making?
5. What are the assumptions about underlying causes of the environmental problem?
6. What criteria are used to evaluate the environmental decision?

suggesting that

> Answers to these and related questions allow us to determine which disciplinary approaches, analytical methods and decision-making tools are most appropriate for evaluating and improving specific decisions. But we must recognise that the categories and sub-categories in Table 2 are artificially systematic and unrealistically precise devices that allow us to construct an easy-to-apply framework for conceptualising the important components of environmental decision making. The simplified framework, whilst useful, cannot completely describe the complexity and interconnectedness of many real-world decisions.

(Sexton et al., 1999, p. 5)

This course will be exploring many of the areas identified by Sexton et al. in the context of a different conceptual framework, which will have the potential to be used both systemically and systematically. However Sexton et al.'s characterisation of environmental decision making gives a useful overview and is used here as just part of our consideration of the kinds of decisions concerned in environmental decision making.

### Activity 5    Engaging with multidimensional characteristics

Look at Table 2 from Sexton et al. (1999):

(a) Are there any words in the table that are not familiar to you? If so, list them in your journal or blog and either look them up in a dictionary or online search, or make a note to come back to them later in the course and see if their meaning has since been made clear.

(b) Sexton et al. use the (underlined) categories of level, domain, setting, mode, assumptions and criteria in grouping dimensions of characteristics of environmental decision making. Work through each category selecting some of the levels, domains, settings and modes you have direct experience of and which assumptions and criteria you have come across before. Given that the list of categories and sub-categories is not intended to be comprehensive, are there any you would add?

## Study note

As with other activities, there is no right or wrong answer to this activity. You may have experience of all or none of the characteristics in this table or somewhere in between. The purpose of this activity is purely to encourage you to engage with some conceptions of environmental decision making and to begin to take stock of your own environmental decision-making experience. My response is provided (as one response, not *the* response) at the end of the book.

Table 2 Multidimensional characteristics of environmental decision making

**I   Social Level of the Environmental Decision**

    1 Individual      3 Organisation
    2 Group      4 Society

**II   Substantive Domain of the Environmental Decision**

A Type of issue

    1 Air quality control
    2 Critical natural areas
    3 Energy production/distribution
    4 Green technologies
    5 Natural resource management
    6 Historic, cultural and aesthetic resources
    7 Urban infrastructure/growth management
    8 Waste management
    9 Water allocation
    10 Water quality control

B Spatial extent

    1 Socially constructed scales, e.g. neighbourhoods, cities, states, countries
    2 Natural system scales, e.g. watersheds, airsheds
    3 Geologically based scales, e.g. plains, valleys, continents, earth

C Temporal factors

    1 Persistence
    2 Reversibility
    3 Cumulative effects
    4 Context (past, current, future decisions)

### III Social Setting for the Environmental Decision

A Key Decision Maker

  1 Individual acting as an independent agent
  2 Individual acting as a member of a group or organisation

B Decision Participants

  1 Governments
  2 Regional governmental organisations
  3 Business associations
  4 Environmental advocacy groups
  5 Community/neighbourhood groups
  6 Affected or interested individuals

C Urgency of decision

  1 Urgent
  2 Deliberative

### IV Modes of Environmental Decision Making

  1 Emergency action
  2 Routine procedures
  3 Analysis-centred
  4 Elite corps
  5 Conflict management
  6 Collaborative learning

### V Assumptions about Basic Underlying Causes of Environmental Problems

  1 Lack of scientific knowledge and understanding about natural systems or impacts of technology
  2 Imbalanced or inappropriate economic incentives
  3 Misplaced belief system and core values
  4 Failure to use comprehensive approaches (overly narrow perspective)

### VI Criteria for Evaluating Environmental Decisions

A Decision process

  1 Fair
  2 Inclusive
  3 Informed

B Decision outcome

  1 Workable
  2 Accountable
  3 Effective
  4 Efficient
  5 Equitable
  6 Sustainable

(Source: adapted from Sexton et al., p. 4)

Figure 5   Some different dimensions of environmental decision making

## 2.4 Environmental decision making in the context of sustainable development

In this course, in simple terms, environmental decision making is taken to mean decision making that has an effect on our environment, however it is defined. If adopting a broad definition of environment, as this course does, it could be said that nearly all decision making comes into this category. So why do we need to talk about environmental decision making at all rather than simply decision making? It is because there is increasing recognition that many of the decisions we make and actions we take, both individually and in groups, have an effect on our environment and yet economic and political considerations often dominate in a way that seems to exclude environmental considerations. By environmental in this context, I mean that which surrounds and affects us including our physical and biological life-support base alongside social, economic, cultural, political and institutional factors.

For the purposes of this course, we shall mainly consider those decisions which have local dimensions but are related to worldwide environmental issues, and where individuals and groups have choices they can make to maximise positive environmental outcomes, improve our environment and limit detrimental effects. Examples include our use of transport, making consumer decisions, planning new or improved developments and managing natural resources.

Whilst accepting that there are widely divergent views about what environmental decision making implies, the T863 Course Team believes that the main challenge seems to be not one of replacing economic, political and social considerations, which currently prevail in much decision making, with an environmental agenda but one of bringing these factors together in every decision-making process. A note of caution is needed however: singling out one area for special attention might on occasions have the effect of separation rather than integration. In order that we might more fully explore this integration of environment with the other factors prevalent in decision making, we perhaps need to begin by taking the position that we cannot afford to exclude environmental concerns if we are to meet basic human needs both now and in the future. This is based on an assumption that the rate at which we are using some of our natural resources (such as oil, water or land) and polluting air, soil, fresh waters and oceans is unsustainable. Hence we will consider environmental decision making in the context of sustainable development and will now go on to explore what that means.

## 2.5 Sustainable development

### Development

'Development' is another term that is used frequently in the context of environmental decision making. Like the term 'environment', it is a word that has many different meanings and understandings. One of its original meanings was as a biological notion synonymous with the natural progression of growth and differentiation to a stage of maturity. It will be used in this course in several different ways:

- In a general sense, to denote progress or the gradual unfolding and filling out, usually used in a positive sense. For example, 'the development of a proposal' or the 'personal development of an individual'.

- To refer to plans. Development plans, which often refer to built structures, have come to have a specific meaning and connotations because in many countries they are subject to legislation and regulation. For example, in the UK development plans are covered in a range of planning acts, regulations and guidance documents including The Planning and Compulsory Purchase Act 2004, The Town and Country Planning (Local Development) (England) Regulations 2004 and The Town and Country Planning (Transitional Arrangements) Regulations 2004 and Planning Policy Statement 12 (PPS12): 'Local Development Frameworks' 2004.
- To describe particular site-based infrastructural projects, such as roads, buildings and dams, in the sense of 'new developments' or redevelopments.
- To refer to 'world' development, where there is also a range of different perspectives:

> Development can be seen in two rather different ways: (i) as an historical process of social change in which societies are transformed over long periods and (ii) as consisting of deliberate efforts aimed at progress on the part of various agencies, including governments, all kinds of organisations and social movements.
>
> (Allen and Thomas, 1992, p. 7)

> Development is not synonymous with economic growth, though the two are often confused. Economic growth refers to a quantitative expansion of the prevailing economic system. Development is a qualitative concept which incorporates ideas of improvement and progress and includes cultural and social as well as economic dimensions.
>
> (Blowers and Glasbergen, 1995, p. 167)

In the context of environmental decision making, the term 'development' is often used with the adjective 'sustainable'.

## Sustainable development

Several events in the 1970s and 1980s emphasised the global nature of environmental issues and the links between environment and development, which in turn led to the emergence of the concept of sustainable development. These events included:

- the production of the World Conservation Strategy in 1980 (by the International Union for the Conservation of Nature (IUCN), the World Wide Fund for Nature (WWF) and the United Nations Environment Programme (UNEP)
- the Brandt Commission on North/South relationships, chaired by the former West German Chancellor Willy Brandt, which reported in 1983
- the World Commission on Environment and Development (WCED), which produced the report 'Our Common Future' in 1987 – also known as the Brundtland Commission, after Gro Harlem Brundtland, the then Prime Minister of Norway, who chaired the Commission. The Brundtland definition of sustainable development became particularly well known:

> Sustainable development is development that meets the needs of the present without compromising the ability of future generations to meet their own needs.
>
> (WCED, 1987, p. 43)

This definition embraces at least three concepts that can be interpreted differently by different individuals: those of development, needs and intergenerational equity.

There have been many more definitions of sustainable development suggested since 1987. Figure 6 is a diagrammatic representation of one that came from the US National Research Council, Policy Division in 1999 (reproduced in Kates et al., 2005).

| WHAT IS TO BE SUSTAINED: | FOR HOW LONG?<br>25 years<br>'Now and in the future'<br>Forever | WHAT IS TO BE DEVELOPED: |
|---|---|---|
| NATURE<br>Earth<br>Biodiversity<br>Ecosystems | | PEOPLE<br>Child survival<br>Life expectancy<br>Education<br>Equity<br>Equal opportunity |
| LIFE SUPPORT<br>Ecosystem services<br>Resources<br>Environment | LINKED BY<br>Only<br>Mostly<br>But<br>And<br>Or | ECONOMY<br>Wealth<br>Productive sectors<br>Consumption |
| COMMUNITY<br>Cultures<br>Groups<br>Places | | SOCIETY<br>Institutions<br>Social capital<br>States<br>Regions |

Figure 6  Definitions of sustainable development

Note: the 'linked by' section in Figure 6 refers to the different emphases in combining what is to be sustained with what is to be developed ranging from 'sustain only' or 'develop mostly' to combinations of what is to be sustained and developed using words such as but, and/or.

## SAQ 2   Concepts associated with sustainable development

List all the concepts included in the definitions of sustainable development given in this section so far, including Figure 6 (by concepts I mean ideas or notions, usually captured by key words or phrases, e.g. 'development' or 'life expectancy').

However it is defined, sustainable development is a concept that has been in use since the mid 1980s and is still very much in evidence. Many people have at least partially accepted it, as was shown by the work done before, during and after the United Nations Conference on Environment and Development (UNCED) – the Earth Summit – in Rio de Janeiro in 1992 and the 2002 World Summit on Sustainable Development (WSSD) in Johannesburg. (I will discuss both of these initiatives later in this section.)

Does it matter that the concept of sustainable development is open to interpretation? Is it important that people share an understanding of this concept or is it more a question of how people use it? Some people consider sustainable development to be a rather vague ideal with implications we have yet to understand, while others have used it to develop clear plans of action with achievable goals.

Here is one view from Sir Martin Holdgate when he addressed the UK Royal Society of Arts in 1995 in his role as President of the Zoological Society:

> My conclusion is that the concept of 'sustainable development' is less novel than has often been made out. It is, in fact, a synonym for 'rational development', because it is a process of making the best practicable use of natural resources for the welfare of people. Its goal must include economic advancement, and there seems no fundamental reason why market economic systems cannot be adapted to generate sound growth while conserving our environment. But the goal of sustainable development is to deliver quality of life, and here we must pause. For there are indefinable qualities in the world that are not easily susceptible to economic valuation, and can easily be swept aside by the tide of expediency. Yet the richness and beauty of nature and the wonder of great landscapes can fill the dullest mind with awe. The development process must value these things, too, and it will indeed be a test of success if a century from now a stable world human population enjoys a quality of life far better than today's average, in a world with something near today's diversity of plant and animal species. It can be done. It will not be easy. The slower we are in adapting the more costly and difficult it will be.
>
> (Holdgate, 1995, p. 25)

Here is another view from Wendy Harcourt from her book *Feminist Perspectives on Sustainable Development*:

> Development = economic growth is at the centre of development discourse. Even though many commentators point out that development is far more than economic growth but extends to social, political, cultural, environmental and gender concerns, economic growth remains firmly entrenched as the stated goal of development from which modern critiques of development begin.
>
> Over the last few years, this approach to development had been criticized and challenged by a number of development economists interested in revising economic theory and methodology to include environmental considerations. They have been joined by development professionals concerned that poverty alleviation and the basic needs approach of development programmes are not bringing about the hoped-for end to mass poverty and environmental deterioration. Women working in development are also part of this debate in their argument that the fundamental gender bias of development thinking and practice prevents gender equity and ignores women's contribution to the economy and their role in the management of

the environment. And radicals in both industrialized and developing countries enter into the debate questioning the whole modernization process and Western knowledge systems on which development is based.

These thinkers and activists have found their voices in the recent policy debates on environment and development labelled 'sustainable development'. They have used the political platform created by the United Nations Conference on Environment and Development (UNCED) ... to bring their particular concerns about the thesis that development = economic growth to the public arena.

(Harcourt, 1994, pp. 11–12)

### Activity 6   What does sustainable development mean?

(a) Read the two quotes from Sir Martin Holdgate and Wendy Harcourt. Make a list of the words or phrases that strike you as particularly relevant to the concept of sustainable development. (You could begin with your answer to SAQ 2 if you find it difficult to start this activity.)

(b) Look at your list and try to group similar or related words together. Write alongside them what train of thought you were following. (Do not try to use all the words.)

(c) Write a couple of sentences about your own perspective in relation to Holdgate's and Harcourt's. Do you identify with any of the points they have made through your own experience?

### Activity 7   Raising questions about sustainable development

Now use your answers to SAQ 2 and Activity 6 to focus on those aspects of sustainable development that raise questions for you so that you can pursue them later in the course. Use one or more spray diagrams to help you clarify, organise and develop your thinking. If you have not used spray diagrams before, first read through the guidelines in the *Techniques* book (Diagramming: Spray diagrams) and/or DVD.

#### Study note

Don't forget to keep a note of your activity responses in your journal as you may need to return to them later.

I have included my own attempt at this activity at the end of this book but yours need not necessarily look the same as mine, as we will probably have different experiences and perspectives.

> ### Box 1  Why use diagrams?
>
> Diagrams have already been used in this book but this is the first time we are asking you to draw your own, which is why this box appears here.
>
> Diagrams can help you to clarify, organise and develop your thinking and to explain to others how you are thinking. They also enable you to represent simultaneous processes or ideas, in a way that is very difficult in sequential prose. They can be used to help simplify and summarise a complex situation, which has the advantage that it can make it easier for others to understand and the disadvantage that in selecting what you include and leave out you over-simplify a situation, which can mislead.
>
> One point to note is that the process of diagramming is often more important than the product. Think carefully about the purpose of your diagram. If it is to be used to communicate your thoughts to other people, you may need to show them the stages you have gone through, not just the final product. Where you have included opinions and judgements for your own purposes, you may need to prepare an edited version before you show it to others. You will also find it helpful to give a meaningful title to your diagrams. You will use diagrams in this course in two ways: firstly by drawing your own; secondly by interpreting those drawn by others. These are two separate but linked skills. Critical consideration of the nature of a diagram drawn by someone else can help to develop your own diagramming. There are many different types of diagram and many different ways in which they can be used. More will be said about these in later books.

## United Nations initiatives for sustainable development and decision making

Out of UNCED emerged conventions on climate change and biodiversity, a set of guidelines of forest principles, a declaration on Environment and Development, and an extensive international agenda for action for sustainable development for the 21st century – Agenda 21. From WSSD came reaffirmed commitment to sustainable development, including a declaration that committed to 'a collective responsibility to advance and strengthen the interdependent and mutually reinforcing pillars of sustainable development – economic development, social development and environmental protection – at local, national and global levels' (the Johannesburg Declaration on Sustainable Development, 4 September 2002). WSSD also produced a plan of implementation. Between these two international Summits came the UN's Millennium Summit when Heads of State adopted a series of goals with targets concerning peace, development, environment, human rights, the vulnerable, hungry and poor, Africa and the United Nations.

These initiatives are inter-related and each has built on what had been done before. Their significance for environmental decision making is that, in common with some other international initiatives, they have attempted to address issues that cannot be addressed at just one level (local, national or regional). National-level programmes (e.g. Local Agenda 21 (LA21) programmes) have been linked to the international level. In all three of the UN Summit processes, concerns about and recommendations for decision making were included.

Agenda 21 was developed well over a decade ago, for UNCED in 1992 (Quarrie, 1992), but it had a long-term horizon with targets for implementation and monitoring of progress and dealing with changing priorities that took place through the United Nations Commission on Sustainable Development. It therefore became an ongoing process and although the language of Agenda 21 is less in evidence now than it was in the 1990s many of the principles and agreements reached in the Agenda 21 process are still relevant.

Agenda 21 was published in some 40 chapters, each presented with a basis for action, objectives, activities and an estimate of financial costs. It had four main focuses:

1 Social and economic dimensions
2 Conservation and management of resources for development
3 Strengthening the role of major (stakeholder) groups
4 Means of implementation

Two chapters to note in the context of this course are:

- Chapter 8, 'Integrating environment and development in decision making', which considers integrating environment and development at the policy and management levels, providing an effective legal and regulatory framework, making effective use of economic instruments and market and other incentives, and establishing systems for integrated environmental and economic accounting.
- Chapter 40, 'Information for decision making', which considers bridging the data gap between the so-called 'developed' and 'developing' worlds, and improving availability of information that could be used for the management of sustainable development.

After UNCED the many recommendations in Agenda 21 were taken up in varying degrees. There was a series of issues around implementation ranging from finance to participation. However, many people worldwide were involved in the overall process of Agenda 21 and it has been a major focus in many different countries for a great deal of activity on environment and development. LA21 programmes were developed in several countries.

In September 2000, at the UN Millennium Summit, 147 Heads of State and Government agreed to a set of development goals, with targets, for combating poverty, hunger, disease, illiteracy, environmental degradation and discrimination against women. These goals became known as the Millennium Development Goals (see Box 2).

A further plan of implementation of action for targeting specific areas of sustainable development emerged from the World Summit on Sustainable Development in 2002.

From the Johannesburg WSSD process came a range of outcomes including:

> The Johannesburg Declaration on Sustainable Development, the official declaration made by Heads of State and Government
>
> The Johannesburg Plan of Implementation, negotiated by governments and detailing the action that needs to be taken in specific areas

Type 2 Partnership Initiatives, commitments by governments and other stakeholders to a broad range of partnership activities and initiatives, adhering to the Guiding Principles, that will implement sustainable development at the national, regional and international level.

(UNEP DTIE website, 2002)

An explicit reference to decision making was made in the Johannesburg Declaration:

We recognize that sustainable development requires a long-term perspective and broad-based participation in policy formulation, decision-making and implementation at all levels.

(Johannesburg Declaration on Sustainable Development (2002, part of point no. 26)

Decision-making processes, including environmental decision making, are implicit in ideas of public–private and other multi-agency partnerships which are mentioned both in the Millennium and the Johannesburg Declarations. As 'Ensuring environmental sustainability' is one of the eight Millennium Development Goals (see Box 2), environmental decision making is also implicit.

## Box 2  The Millennium Development Goals

1. Eradicate extreme poverty and hunger:
   - Reduce by half the proportion of people living on less than a dollar a day
   - Reduce by half the proportion of people who suffer from hunger.
2. Achieve universal primary education:
   - Ensure that all boys and girls complete a full course of primary schooling.
3. Promote gender equality and empower women:
   - Eliminate gender disparity in primary and secondary education preferably by 2005, and at all levels by 2015.
4. Reduce child mortality:
   - Reduce by two thirds the mortality rate among children under five.
5. Improve maternal health:
   - Reduce by three quarters the maternal mortality ratio.
6. Combat HIV/AIDS, malaria and other diseases
   - Halt and begin to reverse the spread of HIV/AIDS.
   - Halt and begin to reverse the incidence of malaria and other major diseases.

7   Ensure environmental sustainability:
   - Integrate the principles of sustainable development into country policies and programmes; reverse loss of environmental resources.
   - Reduce by half the proportion of people without sustainable access to safe drinking water.
   - Achieve significant improvement in the lives of at least 100 million slum dwellers, by 2020.

8   Develop a global partnership for development:
   - Develop further an open trading and financial system that is rule-based, predictable and non-discriminatory. Includes a commitment to good governance, development and poverty reduction – nationally and internationally.
   - Address the least developed countries' special needs. This includes tariff- and quota-free access for their exports; enhanced debt relief for heavily indebted poor countries; cancellation of official bilateral debt; and more generous official development assistance for countries committed to poverty reduction.
   - Address the special needs of landlocked and small island developing States.
   - Deal comprehensively with developing countries' debt problems through national and international measures to make debt sustainable in the long term.
   - In cooperation with the developing countries, develop decent and productive work for youth.
   - In cooperation with pharmaceutical companies, provide access to affordable essential drugs in developing countries.
   - In cooperation with the private sector, make available the benefits of new technologies – especially information and communications technologies.

(Source: http://www.un.org/millenniumgoals/August 2005)

## SAQ 3   Environment and the Millennium Goals

How is the term 'environment' used in the Millennium Development Goals?

How does environmental decision making link up with decision making for sustainable development? Are they the same thing? The short answer is 'No'. For example, a social services department might decide to use more transport to allow more people to have access to basic services. This decision may be in direct conflict with their stated environmental aims to reduce transport-related emissions and yet it is in some ways a sustainable development improvement. This single decision is focused more on social sustainability than environmental sustainability. However, a social services department committed to sustainable development might, as a whole, make a series of trade-offs between environmental, social and economic considerations, so it is misleading to consider the single decision out of context.

I mentioned previously that the focus on environmental decision making in this course is to ensure that environmental considerations are not forgotten. However, I also pointed out the need to integrate environmental, social and economic considerations. In some cases this means that decisions can be made that have positive effects in all three of these areas, such as the win–win situation of an environmental business that provides employment. In other situations it means choices between one aspect and another, involving trade-offs, as in the example of the social services department. Sustainable development is the context for environmental decision making.

In some cases, LA21 programmes were adopted by governments, authorities and organisations that had already developed environmental policies and plans. For instance, nearly all UK local authorities produced LA21 strategies by the end of 2000, although they did vary in form and quality (Webster, 1999). The process they have had to go through to change course from a focus on environment to one on sustainable development has generally been one of moving out boundaries to include a broader range of both people and ideas in decision making. The UK Local Government Act 2000 meant that UK local authorities had a duty to promote economic, social and environmental well-being and sustainable development of their areas in their community planning although they did not have the power to raise money specifically for this activity. The 'systems' concepts and techniques that will be introduced in Book 2 will help to explain this better and show ways in which environmental decision making can take place within the context of sustainable development. The process needs to start with groups of people thinking critically and systemically and working out what is relevant in a particular situation, rather than trying to think about everything at once.

The way that the use of the sustainable development concept has brought people with environmental, social, political and economic agenda into the same forums for discussion and action is a very important part of the context of environmental decision making, and we shall return to it later in the course.

# 3 Values, power and evolving discourse in environmental decision making

## 3.1 The importance of values

The values of decision makers were briefly mentioned in Section 1.3 as a factor that influences decisions. I use value here not in its numerical sense but to mean something that an individual or group regards as something good that gives meaning to life. Values can also be thought of as deeply held views, of what we find worthwhile. They come from many sources: parents, religion, schools, peers, people we admire and culture. Examples of values an individual may hold are those associated with: creativity, honesty, money, nature, working with others.

### Activity 8   Identifying your values

Write down three values that are important to you. Give an example of how one of these values affected your recent decision making.

### Study note

Look at the *Techniques* book (Values: Identifying values) for further detail on how you may identify values and consider how your values affect your decision making.

Values that affect decision making may be collective as well as individual. The following set of values has been identified by a collective process as those underpinning the United Nations Millennium Declaration. They are clearly thought by a group of people, not just an individual, to be important.

### Box 3  Values underlying the Millennium Declaration

The Millennium Declaration – which outlines 60 goals for peace; development; the environment; human rights; the vulnerable, hungry and poor; Africa; and the United Nations – is founded on a core set of values described as follows: 'We consider certain fundamental values to be essential to international relations in the twenty-first century. These include:

- Freedom. Men and women have the right to live their lives and raise their children in dignity, free from hunger and from the fear of violence, oppression or injustice. Democratic and participatory governance based on the will of the people best assures these rights.
- Equality. No individual and no nation must be denied the opportunity to benefit from development. The equal rights and opportunities of women and men must be assured.
- Solidarity. Global challenges must be managed in a way that distributes the costs and burdens fairly in accordance with basic principles of equity and social justice. Those who suffer or who benefit least deserve help from those who benefit most.
- Tolerance. Human beings must respect one another, in all their diversity of belief, culture and language. Differences within and between societies should be neither feared nor repressed, but cherished as a precious asset of humanity. A culture of peace and dialogue among all civilizations should be actively promoted.
- Respect for nature. Prudence must be shown in the management of all living species and natural resources, in accordance with the precepts of sustainable development. Only in this way can the immeasurable riches provided to us by nature be preserved and passed on to our descendants. The current unsustainable patterns of production and consumption must be changed in the interest of our future welfare and that of our descendants.
- Shared responsibility. Responsibility for managing worldwide economic and social development, as well as threats to international peace and security, must be shared among the nations of the world and should be exercised multi-laterally. As the most universal and most representative organization in the world, the United Nations must play the central role.'

(Source: United Nations General Assembly, 2000, Section 1, p. 2)

### Activity 9  Recognising consistency in values

Read through the values underlying the Millennium Declaration in Box 3. Bearing in mind that this is only part of a document, and that objectives to translate these shared values into actions were also listed in the document, do you find that these values are consistent with each other, or not? Write a few sentences highlighting some examples of any consistencies or anomalies you find.

The ways in which values affect decision making can be highly variable. Two people or organisations who espouse the same value such as say 'shared responsibility' may mean quite different things by it and it is common for differences in values to surface in the process of judgement or negotiation rather than in high-level discussions. In environmental decision making, in the context of sustainable development values associated with money may sometimes conflict with other approaches. The case study later in this block provides a good example. The 'costs' of aircraft emissions and noise are considered by many to be more than monetary.

The many ways in which values underpin decision making will be discussed later in the course, for instance in Book 2. Value judgments often lie behind our approaches to decision making. Deciding what to keep, throw away or destroy for instance, whether at an individual or collective level is a process affected by values. Value judgements may become part of a rational process if values are made explicit and at other times may appear to limit rationality, particularly when not made explicit. For instance, someone who explicitly values participatory governance would be expected to pay a lot of attention to who participates in a decision-making process and how. In a rational choice approach to decision making they would explicitly include these aspects in their consideration of a situation. On the other hand, someone who holds this value but does not make it explicit may be perceived as trying to extend or hold up a decision-making process by trying to include more opportunities for participation in less overt ways.

## 3.2 Power relations and sources within decision making

A lot of conceptions of decision making include ideas about power relations. For instance John Heron (1989) identifies three levels of power to be consciously recognised in the process of project or activity design:

1. Hierarchical, with 'power over' leading to 'deciding for'
2. Cooperative, or 'power with', leading to 'deciding with'
3. Autonomous, or 'power to', leading to 'delegating deciding to'

Of course there are many issues associated with each of these categories, for instance in how a process of delegation may be experienced. But the idea is one of an increasingly 'bottom up' rather than 'top down' approach. One outcome of a 'power to' level of power may just be that stakeholders can get on with work or activity rather than waiting for someone else to decide. I have already mentioned, in Section 1.3 some situations where power relations need to be considered in decision making. The two examples mentioned were how or whether people affected by a decision, such as one about a new development, can use their power to influence a decision and how people skilled at using a model use the power associated with their skill (e.g. to explore a context with others or to persuade others to take a particular point of view). Another example is one where some people have more access to and control of information than others because of their role or position. Heron's categorisation could be used to consider each case to consider the power relations among stakeholders.

You will explore these different levels of power in relation to case studies, examples and your own experience in Books 2, 3 and 4 as it can be useful to recognise them in considering questions such as 'Who decides?', 'Who interprets the data?' and 'Who should decide?'

But where does power come from and how can it be generated in constructive ways? Ideas of power sharing or delegating (or not) often appear in news stories, particularly in relation to politics. Do they imply that there is only so much power to go round? Some ideas that may answer these questions come from Gary Klein who wrote a book called *Sources of Power: How People Make Decisions* (1998). Klein wrote this book to try and balance other books that concentrated on the limitations rather than the abilities of decision makers, particularly in difficult conditions. He had done a first study on how fire-fighters make life and death decisions under extreme time pressure and many subsequent studies (including pilots, nurses, military leaders, nuclear power plant operators) as part of a tradition of 'naturalistic decision making' where how people use their experience to make decisions in field settings is considered. Klein and his colleagues found that

> people draw on a large set of abilities that are sources of power. The conventional sources of power include deductive logical thinking, analysis of probabilities, and statistical methods. Yet the sources of power that are needed in natural settings are usually not analytical at all – the power of intuition, mental simulation, metaphor and storytelling. The power of intuition enables us to size up a situation quickly. The power of mental simulation lets us imagine how a course of action might be carried out. The power of metaphor lets us draw on our experience by suggesting parallels between the current situation and something else we have come across. The power of storytelling helps us consolidate our experiences to make them available in the future, either to ourselves or to others.
>
> (Klein, 1998, p. 3)

The criteria for Klein's 'naturalistic decision-making settings' followed those identified by Orasanu and Connolly (1993), i.e. time pressure, high stakes, experienced decision makers, inadequate information, ill-defined goals, poorly defined procedures, cue learning (where patterns are perceived or distinctions made that lead to a next stage), performed within a context of higher-level goals and different tasks with their own requirements, dynamic conditions and team co-ordination.

The following diagram captures some of the ideas that Klein explored.

Klein has written a full book about these sources of power and I cannot hope to capture the richness of that book here. However his diagram, Figure 7, can be thought of as a 'rich picture' (see *Techniques* book, Diagramming: Rich pictures), particularly if considered with his explanation of why he has drawn the diagram the way he has:

> There are many different ways to connect all of these sources of power. Figure 7 presents one framework. Here, the two primary sources of power are pattern recognition (the power of intuition) and mental simulation. That is why they are so prominent. Storytelling seems to rely on the same processes as mental simulation, so it is tucked in next to it. The use of metaphors and analogues seems to rely on the same processes as pattern recognition, except that in pattern recognition the specific metaphors and analogues have become merged, so these two are pushed together. These are the four sources of power that refer to processes, to ways of thinking.
>
> The other three sources of power are based on the first four, so they are arranged further into the periphery. These three refer to activities – ways of using the four processes at the base. Expertise (the power to see the invisible) derives from both pattern recognition and mental simulation. The ability to improvise in solving

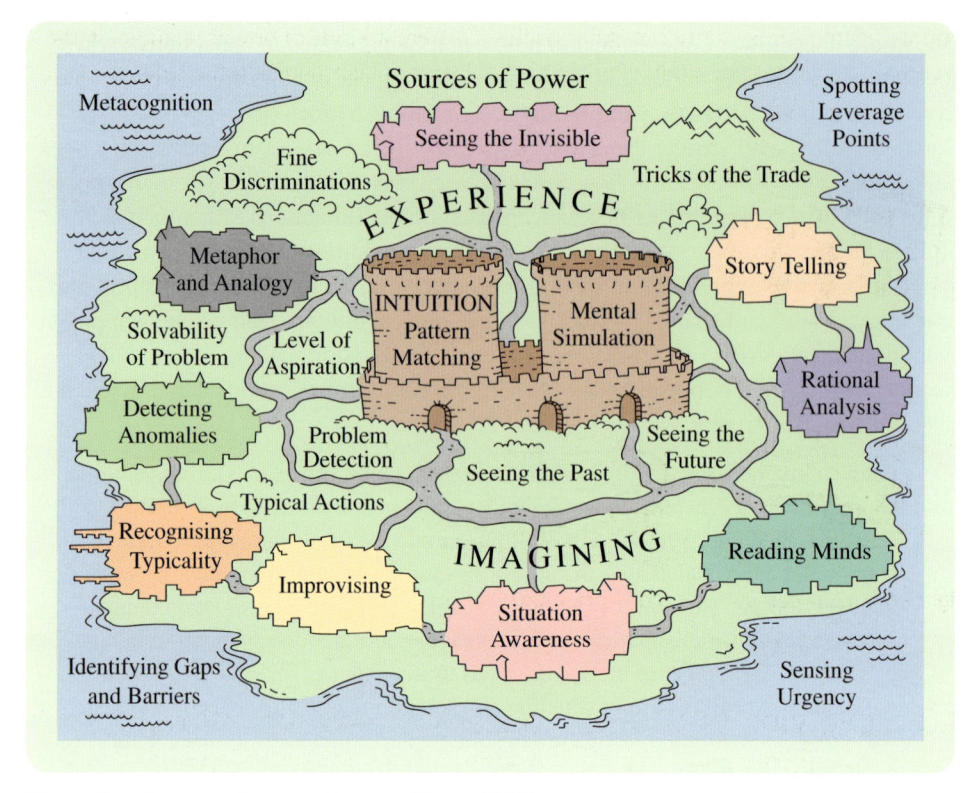

Figure 7  Sources of power (Source: Klein, 1998)

problems also derives from pattern recognition and mental simulation. Our ability to read minds depends on how well we can mentally simulate the thinking of the person. The additional sources of power are arranged according to the same sense of family resemblance. Figure 7 is a concept map of the way I am viewing these processes.

(Klein, 1998, pp. 289–90)

### Activity 10  Sources of power

Take some time to look at the diagram in Figure 7.

(a) Choose one of Klein's 'sources of power' as shown in Figure 7. Write a short account related to your own experience to indicate how you think it could work as a source of power.

(b) What do you find to be missing from Klein's diagram, from your own perspective? Make your own list of 'sources of power' in a decision-making situation familiar to you.

---

In terms of John Heron's three levels of power mentioned at the start of this section, Klein's work is mainly about the autonomous level of power. Many people may be able to draw on, for instance, the power of intuition, storytelling or metaphor to gain insights into a situation. But if working in a hierarchical or even a cooperative context, where power is derived from position or reputation, they may not be able to act to improve the situation.

You will come across more examples of these different kinds of power relations in the aviation expansion case study later in this book and in later books in the course.

Figure 8    (Source: www.cartoonstock.com)

## 3.3 Evolving discourses concerning environmental decision making and sustainable development

What is valued by people and how they think of power relations is often evident in their discourse. A discourse is described by John Dryzek (1997) as 'a shared way of apprehending the world. Embedded in language, it enables those who subscribe to it to interpret bits of information and put them together into coherent stories or accounts'. Discourses change over time as new knowledge and understanding is developed. Individuals also move on to take part in different discourses. For example, from the perspectives of many, the prevailing discourse concerning the relationship of humans with their environments has changed from one of 'mastery over nature' to recognition of the role of people's activities in global warming and depletion of natural resources and the need to manage wastes.

Dryzek developed the following checklist of elements for the analysis of discourses (Dryzek, 1997, p. 18):

1    Basic entities recognised or constructed
2    Assumptions about natural relationships
3    Agents and their motives
4    Key metaphors and other rhetorical devices

Dryzek's category of 'basic entities' acknowledges that different discourses recognise or construct different things in the world. For instance, according to Dryzek, some discourses recognise 'ecosystems', some do not. Assumptions about natural relationships refer to notions of what is natural in the relationships between different entities, e.g. some see competition or cooperation or hierarchies as natural. Agents and their motives refers to both individuals and collectives, mostly human but in some discourses also non-human. Key metaphors and other rhetorical devices are used to refer to one thing in terms of another to put a situation in a particular light.

For instance referring to 'Spaceship Earth' or the 'war against nature' uses the terms 'spaceship' and 'war' metaphorically rather than literally, possibly to invoke a particular image to convince listeners. (You will read more about use of metaphors in environmental decision making in Book 2.)

Dryzek identified environmental discourses around (i) global limits and their denial; (ii) solving environmental problems; (iii) the quest for sustainability; and (iv) green radicalism. All are relevant to environmental decision making in different ways.

For example, he introduced his analysis of 'survivalism' which was a discourse identified in the 'global limits and their denial' in the following way:

> The basic story line of survivalism is clear enough: human demands on the carrying capacity of ecosystems threaten to explode out of control, and draconian action needs to be taken in order to curb these demands. This storyline is in turn constructed from the following basic entities, metaphors, other rhetorical devices, assumptions about natural relationships, agents and motives.

(Dryzek, 1997, p. 34)

Dryzek went on to explain in detail the elements that were part of the story line. He also summarised them (Table 3), which, with a few notes, is sufficient for our purpose here:

Table 3  Discourse analysis of survivalism

| | |
|---|---|
| 1 Basic entities recognised or constructed | • Finite stocks of resources<br>• Carrying capacity of ecosystems<br>• Population<br>• Elites |
| 2 Assumptions about natural relationships | • Hierarchy and control |
| 3 Agents and their motives | • Elites: motivation is up for grabs |
| 4 Key metaphors and other rhetorical devices | • Overshoot and collapse<br>• Commons<br>• Spaceship Earth<br>• Lily pond<br>• Cancer<br>• Computers<br>• Images of doom and redemption |

(Source: Dryzek, 1997, p. 37)

Dryzek describes the elements in this survivalism discourse, as well as listing them in a table. In the summary regarding basic entities, stocks of non-renewable resources (such as oil, coal, etc.) and the capacity of ecosystems to produce renewable resources (such as timber and fish) are treated as finite. The term 'population' rather than people is used to make a point about the aggregate entity, and elites such as governments, modellers, etc. play a central role. In terms of assumptions, there is an assumption that natural relationships are hierarchical and that they can be controlled. In terms of agents, the elites have the capacity to act. Key metaphors and rhetorical devices include 'overshoot and collapse', which refers to population growth of one species at a time (taken from models of the dynamics of simple ecosystems). 'Commons' refers to how we deal with shared resources such as air or fish stocks and to the work of Garrett Hardin (1968) on 'the tragedy of the commons'. 'Spaceship Earth' is a metaphor first coined by Kenneth Boulding in 1966, likening the earth to a spaceship, a whole system. The 'lily pond' and 'cancer' metaphors are linked to ideas of rapid population growth. The 'computer' is an old-fashioned metaphor now for enhanced ability to carry out complex calculations in modelling.

Further details of this environmental discourse and others are given in Dryzek's book.

As mentioned above, this example is just one of many, but it is a useful reminder that our assumptions in or around a discourse can vary a great deal, and it seems reasonable to assume that the nature of the discourse will affect what and who we see as significant in a decision-making process.

### Activity 11 Participating in environmental discourses

(a) Have you participated in or been aware of any environmental discourses before starting this course in the areas that Dryzek identifies? If so, list them.

(b) Give some examples of (not necessarily environmental) discourses you have participated in or been aware of. Do you think these discourses were relevant to environmental decision making?

An analysis of a broader range of discourses concerning approaches to sustainable development has been prepared by Bill Hopwood, Mary Mellor and Geoff O'Brien of the Sustainable Cities Research Institute at the University of Northumbria in the UK (Hopwood et al., 2005).

## Reading 2

Read the paper called 'Sustainable development: Mapping different approaches' by Hopwood et al. (see Study note below) and then answer the following SAQ.

### Study note

You do not need to read the whole of this paper to be able to achieve the learning outcomes for Book 1. It has been provided in its entirety, but if short of time for this reading, you may skim-read some of the detail in the middle section.

> ### SAQ 4  Mapping sustainable development
>
> (a) What kind of shift in understanding do the authors see in the widespread rise in interest in and support for the concept of sustainable development?
>
> (b) Why did the authors use the mapping methodology based on combining environmental and socio-economic issues?
>
> (c) How are the two axes in Figure 1 of the reading labelled? (i.e. what are they plotting against what on this graph/map?)
>
> (d) Which three broad views on the nature of changes necessary in society's political and economic structures and human–environment relationships to achieve sustainable development are overlaid on the Figure 1 map?
>
> (e) What limitations do the authors recognise in their mapping exercise?
>
> (f) In the authors' view, what dominated the sustainable development discourse at their time of writing?

The paper in Reading 2 includes a detailed discussion on what the authors see as the major trends within sustainable development and more extensive conclusions. While the main topic of the paper is sustainable development, it is also highly relevant for understanding discourse on environmental decision making. For instance, the authors analyse and suggest positions for different levels of environmental concern and explicitly consider decision making in the context of sustainable development. They also question what may or may not need to change and the tools and actors needed for these changes to take place.

# 4 Your experience of decision making and environmental decision making

## 4.1 Becoming aware of your actual and potential environmental decision making

In this section you will begin to locate yourself within the overall context of environmental decision making. By considering critically your own experiences of environmental issues in different contexts and at different levels you will begin to consider how people's experiences influence their decisions and actions and how this can be used to positive effect – a theme that will recur throughout the course. Try the following activity now to begin taking stock of your own environmental decision-making experience.

### Activity 12 Your involvement in environmental decision making

In what contexts do you think you are involved in environmental decision making? Give one example of how you are involved individually and one example of how you are involved as part of a group. In both cases explain why you consider them environmental decisions.

---

As individuals it is difficult to understand the nature and scale of the impacts of our decisions, and what we should do about these impacts, because they are part of a large and complex web of interconnected decisions and actions. It is also sometimes difficult to see how the actions of one individual can make a difference, particularly when decision-making processes seem remote and there seems little opportunity to get involved. Figure 9, which shows some factors affecting traffic growth, provides an example.

Nearly all decisions are made by individuals, even when in groups or organisations. We also have multiple roles in society where we are involved in environmental decision making, as consumers, citizens, parents, workers and voters (though not always with awareness), so our decisions and actions can and do make a difference. There are more opportunities to get directly involved in environmental decision making than many people think, although they are not always apparent. The traffic growth example in Figure 9 for instance suggests to me that if I wanted to affect the situation, I could consider how I might, with others, encourage investment in public transport and get involved in improving town planning, as well as reconsidering my own car ownership and avoiding congested times for traffic.

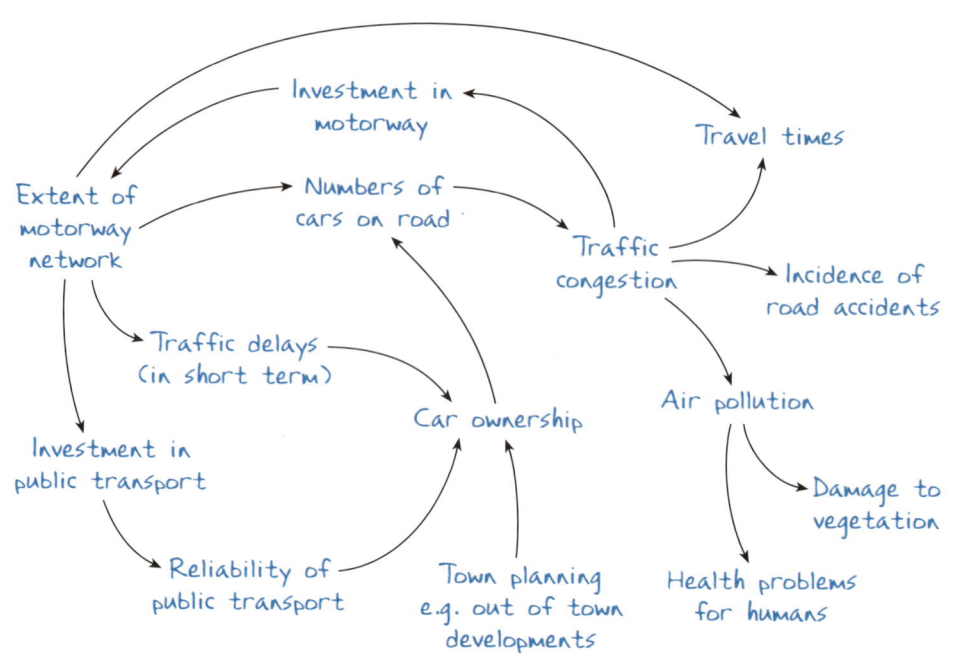

Figure 9  A multiple cause diagram of some factors affecting traffic growth

## 4.2 Different levels of decision making

We make decisions and take actions at a range of different levels: on our own, and within families, communities, nations and international regions. The concept of levels can be useful in working out where decisions are made or should be made.

An example is provided by Norman Uphoff (1992) when considering the types of local institution involved in development activity. See Figure 10, which is also included in a shorter form in the *Techniques* book (see Stakeholder analysis).

The unshaded area in Uphoff's diagram communicates what he means by local institutions. He has drawn conceptual boundaries around ten different levels where decision making and action can occur, ranging from individual to international. By naming and describing the levels he can communicate his understanding to others. He also challenges the way many people use the word local by constructing a boundary around three of the levels – the locality, community and group levels. The distinction is important because, for example, the involvement of local-level institutions is recognised (by Uphoff and others) as essential for mobilising resources and helping to resolve resource management conflicts. Involving just one of the three local levels for decision making may well mean that opportunities to reach a wider constituency are missed. Since this diagram was developed, others (e.g. Buckingham-Hatfield and Percy, 1999) have come forward with even wider understandings of localism. So reaching people at the local level clearly has different meaning for different people.

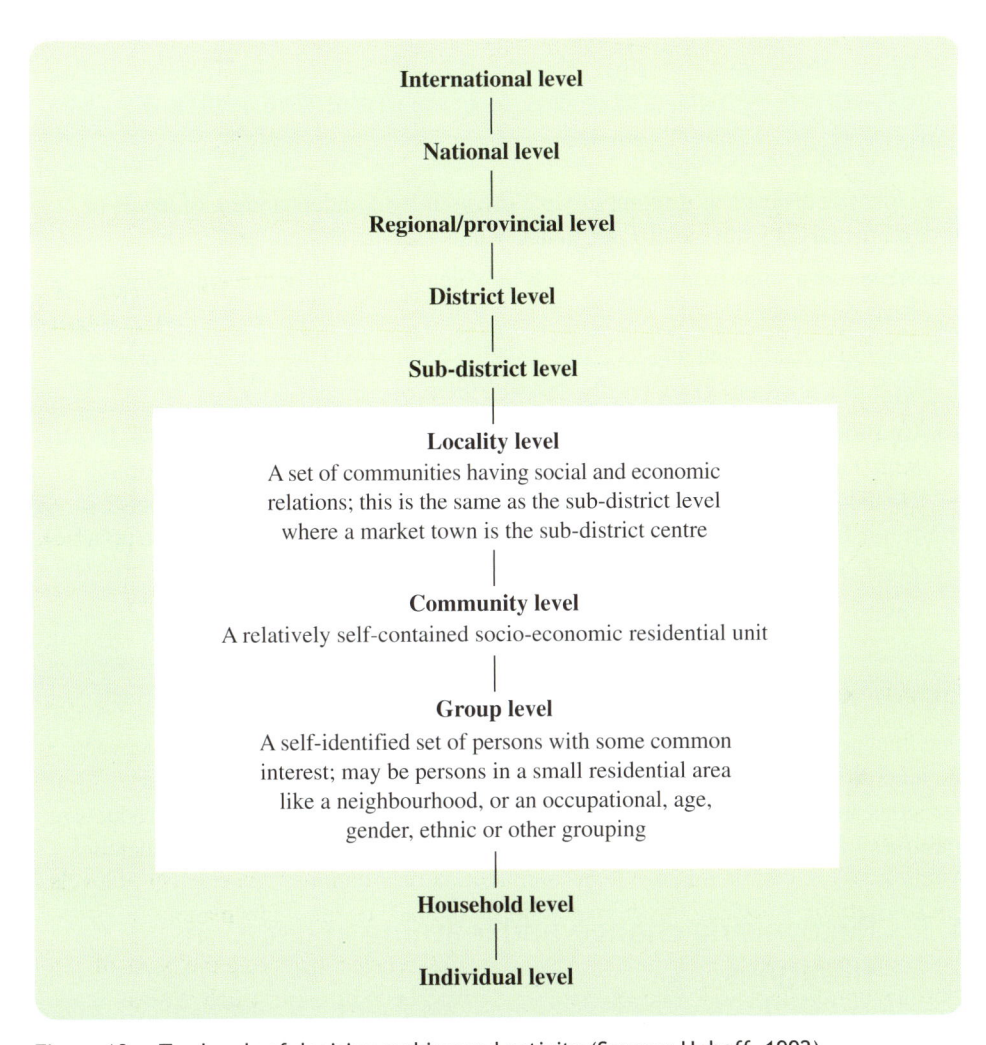

**International level**
|
**National level**
|
**Regional/provincial level**
|
**District level**
|
**Sub-district level**
|
**Locality level**
A set of communities having social and economic relations; this is the same as the sub-district level where a market town is the sub-district centre
|
**Community level**
A relatively self-contained socio-economic residential unit
|
**Group level**
A self-identified set of persons with some common interest; may be persons in a small residential area like a neighbourhood, or an occupational, age, gender, ethnic or other grouping
|
**Household level**
|
**Individual level**

Figure 10   Ten levels of decision making and activity (Source: Uphoff, 1992)

I am using Uphoff's diagram out of context. He went on to give much more descriptive detail and examples of what he meant by the levels in his diagram. He had a particular perspective in that he was writing about local institutions and participation for sustainable development and considering the roles of different organisations and institutions and their effectiveness for natural resource management. The diagram is not necessarily appropriate for all organisations and institutions, particularly where they operate at many different levels. For example, it would be difficult to place a self-identified group of people with some common interest from within one organisation which had several sites (though care is needed in ascribing a perspective to a group as there is likely to be variation within it). Individuals might in that case come from different geographical locations. The group might be predominantly 'local' but the organisation 'regional' or 'national'. However, diagrams can be useful in different ways and Uphoff's diagram is a valuable prompt for considering different levels of environmental decision making. The following is intended to follow on from the activity at the start of Section 4. By all means use some of the same examples, but explore the 'levels' dimensions of them this time.

> **Activity 13  Exploring levels of environmental decision making**
>
> Use Uphoff's diagram as a prompt to explore your own understanding of levels of environmental decision making, particularly at a local level.
>
> (a) Write down some examples of levels at which you are an active environmental decision maker.
>
> (b) Do you identify with any levels of decision making that are not represented on Uphoff's diagram? If so, briefly describe them.
>
> (c) Consider your 'local-level' environmental decision making in more detail. In which local institutions are you involved in environmental decision making? Do they correspond to Uphoff's 'group', 'community' and 'locality' levels? If not, how would you group them?
>
> (d) In what contexts and at what levels would you like to be more active in environmental decision making?

One final point on levels before we leave this section. There is a difference between the level at which we make decisions and the level at which the effects of our decisions are evident. For example, our local decisions to purchase timber products or burn fossil fuels may have an impact at several different levels, from local to global.

## 4.3  Recognising change and learning in decision situations

Decision situations are constantly changing; they are usually dynamic not static. Data on biological and physical processes and human activity, and statements about action being taken to address environmental issues, are obtained at a particular time and in a particular context. Keep in mind that there is a need for caution in interpreting data or statements that originated in a different context or era. Another aspect of change in decision situations concerns learning.

### Experiential learning

Have you ever read a book about a place you have never visited that has meant little to you but returned to the book later after going there to find it meant something quite different?

The same principle can apply when trying to understand the context of your environmental decisions. Accounts of what is happening might well be available but you do not fully understand them. We learn from our own experiences. It is difficult to identify with a problem or an opportunity unless you have experienced some part of it yourself. For example, we can all identify with some activities that have an effect on our environment, such as transport and use of packaging, because we have at least a consumer's perspective. But our experiences may well be very different. For example, people whose livelihood is connected with the transport or food sector are likely to identify with them even more strongly. Identifying with the problem or opportunity is a step towards 'owning' it, but this does not always happen if people do not recognise it as 'their' problem. Recognising that we learn from our experiences is particularly important in environmental decision making because our experiences affect the way we think about a situation, which in turn influences our decisions and actions. This type of learning is an iterative, or recurring, process as illustrated in Figure 11.

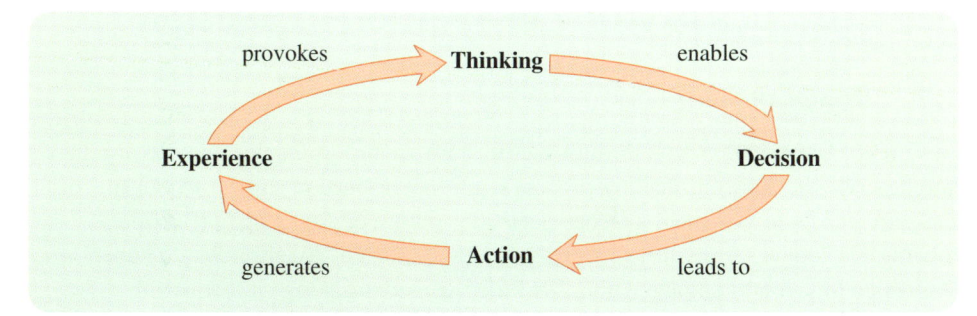

Figure 11  Experiential learning cycle

The experiential learning cycle is just one model of how we learn. This version is adapted to show the place of 'decisions' in the cycle. The original experiential learning cycle was developed by David Kolb and Roger Fry in 1975 (Kolb and Fry, 1975; Kolb, 1984), building on the work of Kurt Lewin, who is better known for his work on action research. As with any model, there are assumptions embedded within it, for instance that the activities identified are the only ones involved in experiential learning and in the order of activities. Other theories of learning have identified other processes. Changes in behaviour, changes in a learner and changes in learners' relationships with others and/or their environments may all provide evidence of learning depending on how learning is theorised (Brockbank and McGill, 1998).

The cumulative environmental impact of individual decisions is often very large, so while each individual's effect may in itself be small, it is still a contributory factor. It is important for all those involved to take responsibility for their actions. In understanding environmental decision making, it is also important to recognise the need to learn and make decisions in groups as well as individually. To be able to do this we need to listen to and try to understand different perspectives as well as just considering our own. This aspect of learning will be discussed in Book 2.

In the context of environmental decision making, learning what changes to make and how at both individual and social levels is important. The importance of social learning and environmental decision making will be discussed in Book 3.

You are now reaching the end of our introduction to environmental decision making and its context, and in the rest of the book you will begin to go into some more depth. In Part 2 you will begin to take stock of some of your own and other people's experiences, thinking, decisions and actions in a detailed case study of a particular sector of environmental decision making – aviation expansion. Before you engage with it, turn to the *Techniques* book and read the section headed Reading a complex narrative.)

# Part Two

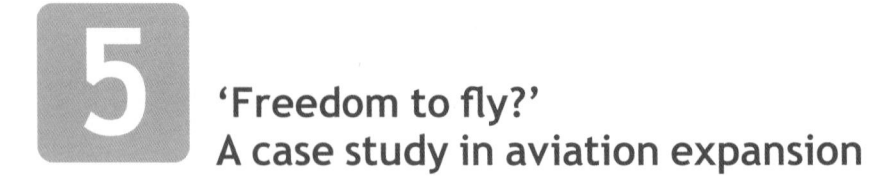

## 5 'Freedom to fly?' A case study in aviation expansion

### 5.1 Introduction

This part of Book 1 takes you through a case study in airport expansion. The aim here is to describe the decision-making process regarding airport expansion with a specific focus on the UK government's December 2003 'Future of Air Transport' White Paper (DfT, 2003a – from now on I will refer to this as the 'Aviation White Paper'). This will allow you to engage with a 'real life' decision-making situation with environmental issues at its heart and build on concepts outlined elsewhere in Book 1. The case study will provide you with an outline of the sequence of events and an interpretation of how they came about. Keep in mind, though, that its purpose is not to teach you about aviation and air transport but to provide you with a rich and complex example of an environmental decision-making process. Take care not to get side-tracked by delving too much into the detail of the case study material.

#### Study note

The principal narrative of this case study is presented as text, but this is supported with a multimedia resource base on the course DVD, including audio and video programmes, digital text, graphs and maps. The text is illustrated with cartoons by Vicky Thompson, a freelance artist. Vicky was asked to engage with the text of the case study, and produced an immediate, intuitive visual response.

I readily volunteered to write this case study because of my personal stake in aviation, living only 15 minutes away from Heathrow Airport in the south east of England, and often jumping at any chance to get out of this relatively cold and wet country (and then enjoying my guilty conscience at leisure on some hot tropical beach). I have to confess that I have only recently begun to take the environmental impacts of aviation seriously. The car was, and probably still is, the environmentalist's transport enemy number one. But the enormous expansion in air travel within the last half of the 20th century, almost doubling every ten years, and the sustained expansion forecast for the first half of the 21st century (see Figure 12) means that major environmental impacts will no longer be limited to the surroundings of international airports. As I write this in 2005, there are over 18,000 commercial aircraft providing in excess of 3 billion passenger kilometres between 1192 airports worldwide. Yet, only 5% of the world's population has ever flown. Reductions in costs and the expansion of airport capacity will allow a significantly greater proportion of the world's population to fly. But at what cost to the environment and to the well-being of those living near airports? Is it time to limit people's freedom to fly?

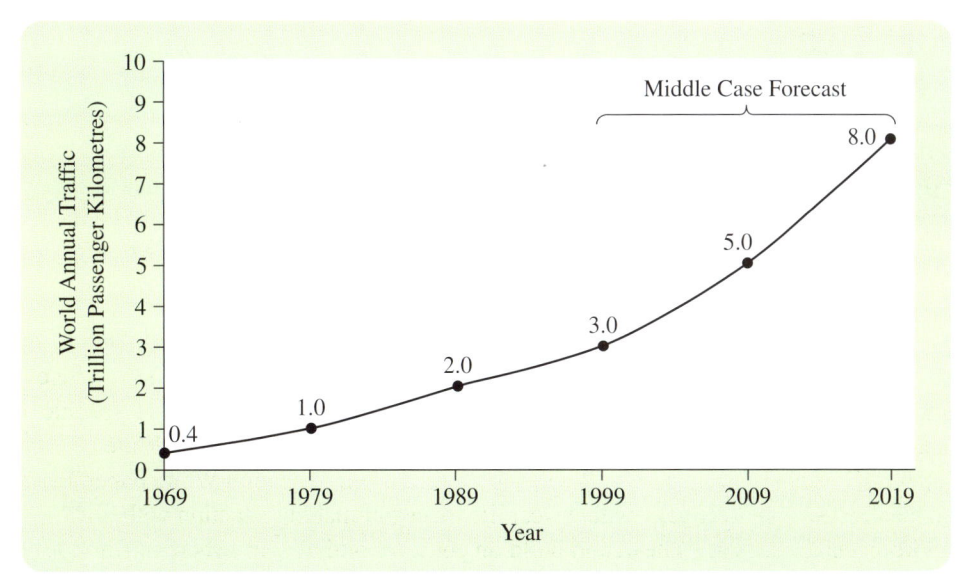

Figure 12 World annual air passenger traffic growth and forecast represented as 'passenger kilometres' (the number of passengers multiplied by the distance of their particular journey). The 'Middle Case Forecast' is the average estimate of growth (Source: ICAO, 2000)

Aviation is one of the most environmentally damaging modes of transport at our disposal today. It contributes to greenhouse gas emissions that are generally accepted as causing global warming. It can adversely affect those living near airports (both in terms of noise and air quality) with many airport workers, especially those in the developing world where health and safety regulations are not as strict and/or implemented, being exposed to toxic levels of exhaust fumes and vaporised fuel chemicals. Airports produce a significant amount of solid and liquid waste and are a drain on surrounding natural resources such as water. But this perspective focuses just on the environmental impacts of aviation. Taking a different perspective, there are significant social and economic benefits. Many people love exotic holidays in far away places, and buy products flown all the way from the other side of the world. Business people in the 'global economy' need to meet face-to-face to clinch deals. And the millions of people employed by the worldwide aviation industry and the associated industries, such as tourism, appreciate the money they receive as a result. The socio-economic demands are such that, if unconstrained, aviation in the UK alone is forecast to double in the next 30 years.

Airport expansion is now a major local issue (for those living near airports) and a global issue (as a result of its increasing contribution to climate change). The Course Team felt that aviation and airport expansion was a good example of a complex, interconnected decision-making situation. But the subject is vast, and in order to provide an example case study with sufficient depth and a clear boundary, we have focused on the decision-making process leading up to the December 2003 Aviation White Paper, a strategy paper published by the UK government (terms like 'White Paper' and other aspects of the UK government's legislative process are explained in Box 5 in Section 5.3). My account of the Aviation White Paper process explores a major event in recent history with environmental decision making at its heart. The Aviation White Paper aimed to set out a strategy for airport expansion in the UK for the next 30 years, while taking into account the environmental impacts of expansion.

### Activity 14 How does aviation affect you?

Before we delve into the Aviation White Paper case study, I would like you to explore how you think aviation is affecting you personally. Below are a series of more detailed questions that may help you explore this. Note your answers in your journal.

- Over the last few years, how many flights do you think you have taken?
- Do you consume or produce any goods that you think require air transportation?
- Who do you think has benefited from your journey and/or consumption?
- What environmental impacts do you think these have had?
- If you are one of the 95% of the world's population that have never flown before, or if you have already flown but feel that you would like to fly a lot more, what constraints do you think are limiting your use of air travel?

### Study note

There's no standard response to this activity, as you will be drawing on your own experience, but to give some examples of points to think about I have briefly included my attempt at this activity at the back of the book. I have selected 2005 as the timescale in which to do this activity.

This activity may help to demonstrate what your personal stake is in aviation. But your decision to fly and/or buy flown-in goods, and the constraints that may limit your flying, are not isolated. They are helped and hindered by other decisions made by other fellow travellers (friends, colleagues, employers), airline companies, airport operators, travel agencies, industries dependent on air transport, environmental non-governmental organisations (NGOs), specialist consultants and a multitude of government departments, to name a few influential stakeholders in air travel. My interpretation of the Aviation White Paper focuses on the process created by the UK government and how the voices of the various stakeholders have been represented (or not).

## 5.2 The need for an Aviation White Paper

Since the liberalisation of air transport within the European Union in the 1980s (the privatisation of airlines and airport operators, and deregulation of air travel, e.g. removal of barriers for foreign airline operations), it was essentially left to the private sector to decide on and fund extra airport capacity. The lack of a national strategy in the UK, and the increasingly vociferous local opposition, meant that any new development was becoming practically impossible. For example, the public inquiry concerning the development of Heathrow's Terminal 5 was the longest in British history. The inquiry lasted for over four years (1995–99) and cost in excess of £80 million (Thorpe, 1999). The aviation industry was therefore desperate to avoid a similar situation in future developments.

*"A SPECIAL BIRTHDAY? I KNOW JUST THE THING..."*

In the year 2000, over 180 million passengers flew from UK airports, with demand to fly having risen threefold since 1980. By 2001, the aviation industry was estimated to contribute £13 billion to the UK gross domestic product (the gross domestic product is a measure of the amount of economic production of a particular nation in financial terms during a specific time period. This is a measure of national income and output, and is frequently used as an indicator of a nation's standard of living). Most calculations of the economic benefits of aviation use a methodology developed by the Federal Aviation Administration, which sums the direct, indirect and induced effects of aviation (I will discuss this in more detail later in the case study). But many UK airports are already nearing their capacity limits especially those surrounding the London area (Heathrow, Gatwick, Stansted and Luton – see Figure 13 for locations). This lack of capacity was seen to severely limit any future growth in passenger numbers and economic gain.

The pressure on the UK government by the aviation industry to provide a long-term strategic plan for air travel is exemplified by the following quote from a regional newspaper:

Figure 13  Map of main London airports

*The Freedom to Fly Coalition combined a wide range of interest groups including airlines, airport operators, trades unions and businesses (represented by the British Chambers of Commerce which has a membership of 135,000 businesses).

Jobs, business, tourism and the economy will all suffer unless aviation capacity increases, a new campaign group said today. The Freedom to Fly Coalition* said the Government must settle the problem of capacity in its aviation White Paper due soon.

(Holmes, 2001, p. 4)

The pressure on the British government to deliver a long-term strategy that guaranteed airport expansion had never been greater.

### Study note

Later on in the course, you will be referred back to the 'Freedom to fly?' case study material many times. Several activities in subsequent books ask you to consider particular aspects of the case study that you will have gleaned from reading, watching and listening to the various case study resources, both in this book and on the DVD. As you watch the video programmes and study the other materials, it's advisable to make notes in your learning journal covering the main themes and key points for your own future reference. The next activity invites you to watch two video programmes from the course DVD. These have been chosen to portray two very different perspectives on the case study topic. Watch them critically. They are not intended to represent the views of the author or the Course Team. Their purpose is to illustrate contrasting positions in the air transport debate.

### Activity 15  Comparing two aviation videos

(a) View the *Reach for the Sky* documentary produced by Undercurrents, an independent media production company. The video will illustrate the local, regional, national and international contexts of air travel and its various environmental impacts, representing many of the issues of concern to the environmental movement.

As you watch the video, try and focus on the social, spatial and temporal dimensions of the various issues presented. Which groups of people are involved? Where are they located? Over which time period are they involved and/or affected? Note your answers to these questions – they may be useful later in the course.

(b) Now, have a look at the video produced by the British Airports Authority (BAA) on *Heathrow Terminal 5*. How does this video compare to the *Reach for the Sky* video in terms of social, temporal and spatial dimensions?

(My response to this activity is at the back of the book.)

---

You should now have a flavour of the contrasting pressures the UK government was under during the Aviation White Paper process and the complex issues of scale that it had to contend with. The next section will illustrate the steps taken by the UK government and the contribution of a range of stakeholders towards the development of the Aviation White Paper.

Activity 15 should have given you an indication of the various scales in operation. At the most basic level, there are individuals deciding whether or not to fly and/or oppose or promote the aviation industry. At a higher organisational level, there are private enterprises who have a financial imperative while at the same time attempting to deal with pressures from clients, shareholders and government (through regulations) (see Box 4). At a more complex organisational scale, there are governments themselves developing national strategies and negotiating at local, regional, national and international level. Although this case study focuses on a national government's decision-making process, the other scales of operation should not be forgotten.

### Box 4  BAA's Environmental Management System

BAA was one of the world's first airport operators to establish an Environmental Management System (EMS) to monitor and control the environmental impacts of its operations. An EMS can be used as a tool to ensure compliance with environmental legislation, where the worst infringements may result in fines, licence revocations and imprisonment. Other benefits of an EMS include cost reductions through increasing efficiency and an improvement in public image. By 2001, BAA had established an informal EMS integrating environmental health and safety management programmes with annual publications stating environmental objectives and targets, which were audited independently. A UNEP/Sustainability Ltd survey published in 2000 identified BAA's EMS as one of the most comprehensive and ambitious in the world (UNEP/Sustainability, 2000). (You will go on to learn more about EMSs in general in Book 2.)

## 5.3 The process leading up to the publication of the UK December 2003 Aviation White Paper

In case you are not familiar with the British government's legislative process, Box 5 briefly describes the role of the 'White Paper'.

### Box 5  The UK's legislative process

The White Paper falls within the first stage of the UK government's legislative process, which is the consultation stage. This includes gathering opinions from experts (e.g. consultants, academia), pressure groups (e.g. industry, NGOs, religious organisations) and the public. There are several motives for initiating a White Paper process, including political party manifestos, international treaties (the European Union being a major source in recent years), proposals from individual Members of Parliament and, finally, proposals from the government itself (which are called 'Green Papers' and are used to gauge interest in initiating the much more extensive and expensive White Paper process). White Papers usually contain detailed and specific proposals for legislation. These documents are therefore the foundation of many legislative bills proposed by the UK government providing factual information, an indication of public support and, finally, guidelines for policy. After the UK government has published a White Paper, then it will either produce a legislative bill and present it to Parliament for debate and/or enact policy changes aimed at facilitating the implementation of the White Paper recommendations. A bill is only necessary if major changes in or additions to existing laws are required. The bill has to be approved by both the House of Commons (elected chamber) and the House of Lords (unelected chamber) before it finally becomes law as an 'Act of Parliament'.

In June 1998, the UK government published a White Paper on land, sea and air transport for the UK called 'New Deal for Transport: Better for Everyone' (DfT, 1998), which announced, among other things, the government's intention to produce a new UK airports policy that would look 30 years ahead.

The new airport expansion process officially started on 12 December 2000, with the publication of the national consultation document 'The Future of Aviation' and the stated intention of producing an Aviation White Paper in a couple of years. This work was initiated by the then Department of Environment, Transport and the Regions. This is now the responsibility of the Department for Transport, DfT, due to a government reorganisation – a reorganisation which, in itself, may have significantly affected the outcome of the Aviation White Paper process, since the new Minister for Transport, Alistair Darling, no longer had 'environment' as an area of direct responsibility.

It is useful to note here that the UK government at that time had only recently taken power. The Labour Party (supposedly of Centre-Left orientation) had swept to power in a landslide victory in the 1997 general election, marking a big change for a country which had previously been dominated by the Centre-Right Conservative Party for almost two decades. The new government was keen to immediately make a mark and so set about implementing a series of reforms, including in the area of transport. Alistair Darling was installed as the Minister for Transport with the brief to radically change the face of UK transport. The Aviation White Paper is reputedly one of his major achievements during his term in office.

Under the leadership of the Department for Transport, the approach to the Aviation White Paper decision-making process had two main thrusts. The first involved detailed research undertaken by private consultancy firms intended to provide the government with objective data. These were often described as 'studies' and were published by the DfT. The second approach involved extensive nationwide consultation with particular stakeholders and the public at large. The DfT had (and still has in 2005) a comprehensive website (www.dft.gov.uk) and provided public roadshows of potential expansion options throughout the process. Consultation responses could either be carried out on paper and posted to the DfT or submitted online.

Table 4 shows the Aviation White Paper timeline, starting with the publication of 'The Future of Aviation'. Each major step in the decision-making process is marked by the publication of key documents. As you will see, the studies and consultations did not always follow each other in a logical sequence.

Table 4  The Aviation White Paper timeline

| | |
|---|---|
| July 1998 | The White Paper, 'New Deal for Transport: Better for Everyone', announced the government's intention to produce a new UK airports policy that would look 30 years ahead. |
| March 1999 | UK government announced plans to produce a national consultation document and to commission several regional studies on airport expansion. |
| December 2000 | Release of national consultation document, 'The Future of Aviation', and the following supporting papers:<br>● 'UK Air Freight Study – Part 1' (DfT, 2000b);<br>● 'A Study into the Potential Impact of Changes in Technology on the Development of Air Transport in the UK' (DfT, 2000c);<br>● 'Valuing the External Costs of Aviation' (DfT, 2000a);<br>● 'Air Traffic Forecasts for the United Kingdom' (this document provided the estimates for future demands which underpinned the consultation documents) (DfT, 2000d). |
| April 2001 | End of consultation period on national consultation document. 550 responses received. |
| | Regional studies to assess the potential for and impact of airport expansion initiated in seven UK regions, including the South East and East of England Regional Air Services Study (SERAS) and the Regional Air Services Coordination Study (RASCO), which summarised the results of the six regional studies excluding the South East and East of England. |
| November 2001 | Summary of national consultation responses released on DfT website. |
| July/August 2002 | Seven regional consultation documents, based on the regional studies, were published collectively as 'The Future Development of Air Transport in the United Kingdom' (DfT, 2002). Alongside the seven consultation documents, the government commissioned seven questionnaires which asked for views on issues covered in the consultation documents. Over 66,000 completed questionnaires were received. Consultation events and exhibitions were also held across the UK. |
| November 2002 | Deadline for submission to regional consultations extended to June 2003 by High Court ruling. |
| March 2003 | Publication of 'Aviation and the Environment: Using Economic Instruments'. |
| June 2003 | Close of consultation period on regional consultation documents. |
| December 2003 | Publication of Aviation White Paper, The Future of Air Transport (DfT, 2003a), and supporting documents, including a Regulatory Impact Assessment and the South East report on responses to the government's consultation. |

## Study note

The DVD contains the same timeline table but with the document titles hyperlinked to copies of the original documents. For example, 'The Future of Aviation' document was supported by two key publications: the 'Air Traffic Forecasts for the United Kingdom' and 'Valuing the External Costs of Aviation'. All of these can be found on the DVD. You may want to familiarise yourself with the timeline and associated reports. There is, however, no need to read all the reports in detail. These have been included in the DVD to give you access to the actual studies and consultations just in case you are interested in exploring the original material used within the decision-making process.

### Activity 16  Contextualising the Aviation White Paper timeline

In order to contextualise the timeline with worldwide events, several television news clips are included on the DVD. They are shown in an additional column within the DVD timeline table. View these clips and then produce your own notes, as if you were adding another column on the timeline that describes your own personal experiences and awareness of aviation-related events. I provide my own response at the back of the book.

As you go through the remainder of the case study, see if you can identify influences of worldwide events on the Aviation White Paper process.

## Structuring the decision-making process

From the start of the process, the British government saw the issue as an attempt to 'maximise the significant social and economic benefits that growth in aviation would bring' whilst minimising or 'paying for' the environmental impacts of such development (as quoted in 'The Future of Aviation').

The UK government decision-making process on airport expansion posed the following three fundamental questions:*

1. How much extra airport capacity (defined as the number of passengers embarking on a flight per annum) will be needed over the next 30 years?
2. How will the environmental impacts be mitigated or paid for?
3. Based on the forecasted passenger number, where should the new airport capacity be located?

*This structure is not immediately apparent in the DfT documentation but has been interpreted in this way by most commentators in the media, although many have placed the environmental impacts as the last question.

### Activity 17 Considering questions that framed the process

The posing of these three questions had a fundamental impact on the decision-making process, imposing limitations on the scope of the studies and the consultations, and effectively predefining the outcomes. Can you think of a different set of questions which could have framed the process in a better way?

---

As I describe the consequences of structuring the decision-making process with these three questions in the remainder of this case study, I will also provide other alternatives proposed by a range of stakeholders, some of which challenged both the process undertaken and the data provided. You may want to compare your response to the above activity with other stakeholder reactions, and to the course material as you engage with it.

### How much airport capacity?

The purpose of the UK government's 'Air Traffic Forecasts for the United Kingdom' report (DfT, 2003b), published at the same time as the 'The Future of Aviation' document, was to present the passenger demand forecasts as a means of structuring the investigation into options for airport expansion. A private consultancy company, Halcrow, was contracted to work on the DfT's forecasting models: Second Passenger Allocation Model (SPAM) and then Second Passenger Allocation Simulation Model (SPASM).

### Study note

I would like to repeat here the same warning mentioned in my response to Activity 14 (at the back of the book) about the carbon emissions calculations. Although seemingly very complex, these mathematical models have to make significant simplifications and therefore cannot possibly take into account every possible parameter which will determine actual passenger numbers. Yet, these played a significant role in the decision-making process. Books 2 and 3 will look at modelling in more detail.

By 2001, Halcrow had acquired sufficient data to provide a long-term simulation of passenger numbers. The SPASM forecasts of airport capacity produced by Halcrow included several assumptions on the fundamental drivers of long-term air traffic levels. These included:

- people's increasing desire for travel;
- an optimistic outlook for the future health of the UK and the global economy;
- the UK's increasing attractiveness as a global tourist destination;
- an acceleration in the globalisation of industry, capital and labour;
- increased liberalisation of the air transport industry and competition;
- the limits of substitutability of alternative modes of transport, such as rail;
- a reduction in the cost base, pricing and operational strategies of the aviation industry;

5 'FREEDOM TO FLY?' A CASE STUDY IN AVIATION EXPANSION

- the increasing competition from hubs in mainland Europe and elsewhere;
- the short-term duration of the effects of shocks (such as the terrorist attacks on 11 September 2001);
- the stabilisation of oil price around $25 a barrel.

You may briefly want to assess how reasonable you feel these assumptions might be. The 'national consultation' section below shows that a concerted challenge on these assumptions by a range of stakeholders opposed to aviation expansion was made.

Based on these assumptions, the SPASM model outputs recommended a medium-term forecast of 500 million passengers by 2030 (as opposed to 180 million passengers who flew in 2000). The DfT concluded in the 'Future of Aviation' consultation document that 'the overall forecast of 500 million passengers in 2030, assuming airport capacity is accommodating, should be robust' (DfT, 2003a, p. 5). Thus the government's forecast was that demand will almost double within the next 20 years.

THE SPASM-ATRON ™ — PERFECT FOR YOUR EVERY NUMBER-CRUNCHING NEED!

## How will the environmental impacts be mitigated or paid for?

As major expansion was now seen as inevitable by the government decision makers, the issue of aviation's environmental impacts had to be dealt with. Any study and/or valuation of environmental impacts by the aviation industry had to take into account the following key issues:

1. Noise – this is the single most important issue at the local level. Although significant improvements in aircraft engine design have resulted in drastic noise reductions, the sheer quantity of take-offs and landings is still causing levels of

distress for people living near airports. Prolonged exposure to high levels of noise has been shown to cause loss of concentration during the daytime and sleep deprivation at night, sometimes leading to heightened stress levels and a reduction in immunological defences.

2   Emissions – these result not only from the aircraft themselves, but from ground support vehicles, refuelling and power generation equipment, and the extensive transportation infrastructure required to bring people and goods to and from airports. These create air quality problems locally and contribute to climate change globally. To the latter, one can add the potentially significant effects of condensation trails (contrails for short). These are the plumes of cloudlike condensation left behind in the atmosphere by passing aircraft. These plumes contribute to the reflection of heat back to earth and could contribute significantly to global warming. The particular chemicals involved include nitrous oxides, volatile organic compounds (VOCs), sulphur dioxide, ozone, small particles which contribute to health problems in the immediate surroundings of the airports and $CO_2$ as a major contributor to greenhouse gases in the atmosphere.

3   Water quality – on-site aviation industrial activities such as aircraft de-icing, maintenance and refuelling can cause the contamination of surface and groundwater. This could potentially affect the health of humans and other organisms directly by polluting drinking water supplies, or indirectly by incorporation into the food chain.

4   Waste – in-flight catering and toilets, along with extensive terminal facilities, generate significant amounts of liquid and solid wastes. These require large-scale treatment facilities which, if unavailable or malfunctioning, could threaten human health and the surrounding environment.

5   Land-take – this is probably the least publicised environmental impact, but the building of new runways, terminals and access infrastructure, and indirect development as a result of the economic stimulation, may result in additional pressure on green spaces which are already scarce, especially around already heavily urbanised areas such as London.

> ### Box 6   Greenhouse gases and climate change
>
> Greenhouse gases, including water vapour ($H_2O$), carbon dioxide ($CO_2$), methane ($CH_4$) and nitrous oxide ($N_2O$), have the effect of warming the global climate. Without them, the earth's temperature would be considerably colder than it is now. The gases allow radiation from the sun to pass through, but they reflect some of the heat that radiates back from the earth's surface. An increase in atmospheric concentration of these gases increases the reflective ability of the atmosphere and thus results in higher global temperatures. Different gases have different reflective properties. For example, a kilogram of methane is 23 times more powerful at reflecting heat back to earth than a kilogram of carbon dioxide, while nitrous oxide is 296 times more powerful. So when estimating the impacts of these emissions, it is not only the quantities released into the atmosphere that have to be taken into account, but also their reflective power.
>
> The major contribution of air travel to greenhouse gas emissions is $CO_2$. Air travel currently accounts for 3.5% of $CO_2$ emissions, although the 'Aviation and the Global Atmosphere' study carried out by the Intergovernmental Panel on Climate Change in 1999 shows that the effect could be three times more potent as a result of the emission directly into the upper atmosphere.

"AND AS PART OF OUR LAND-TAKE COMPENSATION SCHEME, WE ARE GIVING OUR PLANES A 'WETLAND' LIVERY..."

So how should the government ensure that aviation meets the external environmental costs for which it is responsible? Should greater emphasis be placed on regulation (at global, national or local level), economic instruments or voluntary agreements? The 'Valuing the External Costs of Aviation' document set out the government's fundamental approach to tackling environmental issues:

> Under the polluter pays principle, external costs should be reflected in costs incurred by the aviation industry, so that (in an ideal world) it fully meets its external costs.

(DfT, 2000a, p. 1)

The 'polluter pays principle' basically implies that whoever causes pollution is responsible for the costs of repairing any damage. The 'external costs of aviation' are therefore an attempt to quantify in monetary terms the costs of repairing or compensating for the environmental impacts listed above.

The following is an example of how the government proposed to meet the 'external environmental costs':

> Monetary values for the effects of noise were estimated by assessing the impact of increased air traffic noise on house prices in the region of the airport option. The tentative finding of past research, that a 1 decibel* change in noise level results in an approximate 0.5 to 1 per cent change in house prices, was used to estimate the order of magnitude of the noise value of different options. Values at Heathrow ranged between 36 and 40 pence per passenger; at all other airports in the South East, values never exceeded 5 pence per passenger.

(DfT, 2003a, p. 102)

The 5 pence levy per passenger for all the airports in the south east of England (except for Heathrow Airport), was seen to represent adequate compensation for the disruption caused to residents surrounding the airports and would be included in the ticket price for those journeys leaving from the south east of England. A higher charge would be placed on tickets leaving from Heathrow.

*A decibel is a measure of the loudness of sound. A value of 0 dB is at the threshold of human hearing while values above 85 dB are considered harmful to human hearing. Many aeroplanes are capable of producing 100 dB at a 170 m distance.

The other significant environmental impact that was converted into monetary costs by the report was climate change as a result of $CO_2$ emissions. The valuation of climate change impacts as a result of $CO_2$ and other greenhouse gas emissions is an extremely problematic and controversial area, with estimated costs ranging from £3 to £120 per tonne of carbon, and £1500 to £2400 per tonne of nitrous oxide. These upper and lower limits are constantly changing as scientists argue on the effects of global warming – for example the influence on the frequency of hurricanes in the USA, droughts in Africa and floods in Bangladesh. The values in Table 5 show the estimated monetary costs (in pounds sterling) for different aircraft types, i.e. the values represent the estimated costs of environmental damage caused by each journey for each aircraft type (short-haul journeys represent domestic and European travel while long-haul journeys represent extra-European travel such as to the USA or Asia). You can see that the values differ greatly between high and low estimates, yet the DfT required a single value for short-haul and long-haul flights to be passed on to the ticket price, so a weighted average was taken of the 'medium' figure reflecting the proportion of different aircraft types using UK airports and the proportion of short-haul and long-haul operations.

Table 5  Damage costs per journey in pounds sterling as a result of climate change impacts from aviation emission according to aircraft type and journey distance.

| Short-haul operations | | | | Long-haul operations | | | |
|---|---|---|---|---|---|---|---|
| Aircraft type | Low cost (£) | Medium cost (£) | High cost (£) | Aircraft type | Low cost (£) | Medium cost (£) | High cost (£) |
| Boeing 737-400 | 106 | 211 | 422 | Airbus 340 | 1768 | 3536 | 7072 |
| Airbus 320 | 127 | 254 | 508 | Boeing 747-400 | 2486 | 4972 | 9944 |
| McDonnell-Douglas 82 | 150 | 300 | 600 | Boeing 767-300 | 1223 | 2445 | 4890 |
| Boeing 757 | 184 | 368 | 736 | Boeing 777 | 1886 | 3771 | 7542 |
| Airbus 310 | 166 | 331 | 662 | | | | |

(Source: DfT, 2000a)

Other impacts, such as those on water quality, waste and land-take, were seen to be either insignificant and/or too complex to quantify economically. So it was decided to assess these impacts qualitatively by allowing experts to draw up a list of criteria on the importance of, say, the landscape surrounding airports, and then for the same experts to assign an index value along a five point scale ranging from 'low impact' to 'high impact'. For example, if the areas lost to airport development contained a low biodiversity, then the ecological effects of development would simply be described as 'low impact'. This is in stark contrast to the apparently precise monetary figures calculated for noise and emissions impacts.

Thus, the 'Valuing the External Costs of Aviation' report dealt with the environmental impacts (chiefly the effect of aviation emissions on climate change) by proposing to internalise the total environmental costs by eventually adding an approximate £3 levy on short-haul flight costs and a £20 levy on long-haul flight costs per passenger. It was assumed that the 'stimulus to demand from the growth of low cost airlines and from increased airline competition could be sufficient to offset the suppressing effect [on passenger numbers] of any new environmental charges'.

"A BEAUTY, SIR! ONE CAREFUL OWNER, AND IN ONE OF THE LOWEST ENVIRONMENTAL DAMAGE COST BRACKETS..."

But none of the research explained in detail how the funds raised would be used to repair and/or compensate for the various environmental impacts of airport expansion and associated effects. Some suggestions included paying for schoolchildren surrounding airports to have regular day-trips to 'quiet' areas to compensate for the daily disruption they experienced as a result of the aircraft noise. Other questions were left unanswered, for example how the levy was going to compensate the millions of people potentially affected by aviation's contribution to climate change.

### Response to national consultation

'The Future of Aviation' consultation ended on 12 December 2000 and over 550 responses were received, with 120 responses from individuals, 106 responses from local authorities, 72 responses from environmental and residential organisations, and 119 responses from airports, airlines and related aviation organisations.

The overwhelming response to the questions about the environmental impacts of aviation was that the 'polluter should pay' and that aviation should meet its full 'external environmental costs' without benefiting from government subsidies. The taxation of aviation fuel was a major issue raised, although it was felt that this should be agreed at international level by the International Civil Aviation Organisation (ICAO) (many respondents thought noise and emission standards should also be set by ICAO). Several respondents also said that value added tax (VAT) should be charged on air travel and on the purchase of aircraft. They pointed out that the British government was indirectly subsidising aviation by not taxing aviation fuel. In the mid 20th century, when the international airline industry was beginning to develop, tax had been construed as a major source of conflict as different national governments could charge different levels of tax, especially on fuel, potentially placing national airlines at a disadvantage. So in 1944, during the Chicago Civil Aviation Conference, an international agreement was made to not charge any tax on aviation-related businesses, including aviation fuel and the cost of aircraft. In 1992, the USA introduced the Open Skies Agreement which further liberalised aviation and made it virtually impossible for any national government to unilaterally introduce taxation on aviation.

Some specific responses that challenged both the assumptions and processes outlined in the national consultation document are included below.

> Airport Watch, a coalition of major environmental NGOs, including Friends of the Earth, Transport 2000 and the Woodland Trust, saw things very differently. The NGOs suggested that a tax on aviation fuel would effectively bring to an end the rising demand for air travel.
>
> Friends of the Earth and other NGOs were able to re-run SPASM with the same fuel VAT charges as those on cars (17.5%). The additional increases in travel costs effectively resulted in a significantly reduced number of passengers, rising to 315 million by 2030, and not the 500 million as predicted in the original simulation. This meant that existing runways could accommodate the increase if all capacity was used throughout the United Kingdom – no new runways would have to be built.
>
> Many groups also began to question the other assumptions made in the original SPASM simulation. For example, at the time of writing this case study in 2005, the price of oil seems to be 'stabilising' at around $65 per barrel, more than double the price originally used, and this is only four years after the original estimate.

Another major criticism was aimed at the decision-making process. At no stage were limiting factors such as $CO_2$ emissions considered. UK emissions of $CO_2$ in 2001 were 572 million tonnes, with aviation contributing 30 million tonnes (DTI, 2003). The Department for Trade and Industry 2003 Energy White Paper set a target of reducing total UK carbon emissions by 60% by 2050. Taking this target into account, it is estimated that the UK's carbon emissions will be reduced to 495 million tonnes by 2020. The emissions resulting from the aviation growth forecasts by the original SPASM simulation would result in a projected 77 million tonnes of $CO_2$ released into the atmosphere by 2030, almost 16% of the total allowable emissions. The implications are that the UK population would have to drastically cut $CO_2$ emissions by, for example, reducing car journeys, household heating, and developing renewable and nuclear energy sources, just in order to accommodate the significant growth in emissions from air travel. So not only is aviation subsidised by not paying tax on fuel, but the non-travelling population would have to make additional sacrifices to accommodate the expansion, if the Energy White Paper supposed targets are to be met.

### Activity 18  Comparing audio interviews

The audio programme titled *Leading up to the White Paper* on the DVD contains two interviews – one with Mike Fawcett and Chris Cain of the Department for Transport and the second with Peter Ainsworth MP. Mike Fawcett was head of the Airports Policy Division from September 1996 until December 2003 and had overall responsibility for the production of the Aviation White Paper. Chris Cain worked in the Airports Policy Division from 1999 and was responsible for devising, commissioning and managing the programme of preparatory studies, preparing and undertaking some of the public consultations, and drafting sections of the White Paper itself. Peter Ainsworth was chair of the Environmental Audit Committee (i.e. a UK parliamentary committee) at the time the White Paper was published. The committee's remit is 'to consider to what extent the policies and programmes of government departments and non-departmental public bodies contribute to environmental protection and sustainable development'.

The two interviews present distinct views on the context leading up to the Aviation White Paper and on the process itself. Listen to these interviews and contrast them to your response to Activity 17. Compare your intuitive assessment as a newcomer to the issues with that of people who have been intimately associated with the process.

No response is provided as I am unable to take a newcomer's perspective here.

## Where should the new airport capacity be located?

While the 'Future of Aviation' consultation was going on and various stakeholders were coming to terms with the associated reports, the DfT also initiated seven Regional Air Service (RAS) studies, to assess the possible locations for airport capacity expansion and to evaluate the various economic, social and environmental impacts. These regional studies did not take into account the responses from national consultation, but were entirely based on the estimates of passenger numbers and on the 'Valuing the External Costs' approach proposed by the December 2000 documents.

One of these RAS studies was the South East and East Regional Air Service (SERAS) study which was announced in March 1999. Figure 14 shows the geographical coverage of the SERAS study. Right from the start, SERAS was considered to have a significantly greater challenge compared to the other regional studies. The South East has the largest airports in the UK, is considered to be the country's economic powerhouse and has the highest population density. Crucially, approximately 80 per cent of UK passenger traffic has an origin or destination in the south east of England. (DfT, 2002).

Figure 14  Location of South East region within which SERAS study was based

Any decision on airport expansion would need to consider the South East very seriously. The only other area identified for significant expansion was the West Midlands where the main options were a brand new airport between Rugby and Coventry, or expansion at Birmingham and the East Midlands airports. In the rest of the country, the Regional Air Service studies outlined a policy of making full use of existing airport capacity.

SERAS included a comprehensive scoping, evaluation and decision-making framework to deal with the difficult issues specifically related to the south east of England. The approach was based on a relatively recent development by the UK government under the umbrella of 'multi-modal studies'. This involved an explicit analysis of the interactions between all modes of travel and between land use and transport. Investments in infrastructure, services and policy were given equal weighting and were evaluated against environmental, safety and economic impacts. The studies were undertaken by independent consultants with a wide range of skills and submitted to the relevant government body. As this methodology was developed for land surface travel, the Regional Air Service studies had to develop their own particular approach.

## The SERAS process

The specific aim of the SERAS process was to examine the various airport expansion options for the South East over the next 30 years. Figure 15 shows the location of the existing and proposed airports in the south east of England.

Figure 15  Location of existing and planned airports within the south east of England according to SERAS, also showing the county boundaries within which these are situated

Each site was assessed according to the following three categories:

- no development beyond that already envisaged in the land-use planning system;
- development of airport terminal capacity to make full use of existing runway capacity;
- development of additional runway and terminal capacity.

Another significant component of the framework was that any airport development had to be seen to be funded by the private sector, so the interests shown by businesses were going to play a major role in influencing the location of the expansion.

The framework was implemented in five stages within SERAS: a search for sites (Stage 0); a selection of various site combinations to accommodate the various capacity forecasts (Stage 1); an appraisal of the options (Stage 2); more detailed studies on the most promising options (Stage 3); and finally, the making of a case for the most favourable options (Stage 4).

The aim of Stage 0 was not only to look for expansion of capacity within existing airports, but also to look for new sites within the South East which could accommodate a major new airport. Expansion on the existing airports was seen to be increasingly problematic due to the high surrounding population densities (chiefly Heathrow) and the repeated promises that no further expansion would occur after several major developments in the 1980s and 1990s.

> "SEE, IF WE JUST EXTEND THIS RUNWAY TO MANCHESTER, THEN WE DON'T ACTUALLY HAVE TO TAKE OFF AT ALL, THEREBY CUTTING EMISSIONS AND SAVING FUEL..."

The most promising new site was identified at Cliffe in North Kent, which was proposed as a major international 'hub' airport with a total of four runways, compared to Heathrow's two. This would provide a significant amount of capacity in an area with very low population density. The site would be situated on a marsh on the edge of the Thames estuary and would involve construction over several nature reserves.

Stage 1 then went on to identify the feasibility of development on existing and new sites. This analysed the sites on an individual basis, while Stage 2 went on to combine the various sites so as to identify the options with the lowest cost–benefit ratio.

In Stage 3, the most promising options were selected for further analysis. An attempt was made to first identify the level of environmental impact, and then to quantify the environmental costs of expansion. These included a consideration of the effect of noise, local air quality and global warming and how these could be 'paid for' by increasing air fares. Other factors considered in Stage 3 included surface transport, safety, land-and property-take, heritage, ecology, landscape, urbanisation and employment. This resulted in revisions to runway layouts, supporting infrastructure and recalculation of expected capacity for the various options.

The SERAS framework made no attempt to balance the environmental and economic impacts, or find a compromise between the various stakeholders at national and local level. Its aim was to reveal the objective 'facts' on airport expansion within the south east of England, and for these to be assessed in a regional consultation, and eventually, by government ministers.

Table 6 shows the resulting cost–benefit analysis for the various options. The 'cost–benefit analysis' technique is explained in the *Techniques* book (Economic evaluation: Cost–benefit analysis) and the SERAS cost–benefit analysis will be studied in more detail in Book 3. The central objective of SERAS was to provide a robust financial appraisal of various expansion options that would ultimately allow a monetary comparison and a decision on the most cost-effective option. Economic and financial appraisal was conducted over the period to 2030, so that the effect of increasing airport capacity could be assessed year by year over the life of the new infrastructure.

In order to compare options, a number of assumptions were made about how each new runway scheme might be taken forward. Outline layout plans were produced for terminal and other facilities as well as an assessment of the road and rail infrastructure needed to support the airport development. A date for the opening of each runway was assumed. The capacity of different airport options was estimated and forecasts produced of how many passengers would use the new facilities. This enabled an estimation of the cost of construction and a measure of the impacts on people and the environment. For example, meeting the costs of carbon dioxide emissions would increase the costs within the cost–benefit analysis by about £1 billion (Cliffe), £1.5 billion (Stansted, three runways) and £2.5 billion (Heathrow, one runway, and Stansted, two runways).

The SERAS study also used the Federal Aviation Administration methodology for calculating the economic benefits of aviation expansion. Direct impacts were estimated by assessing the increased economic activity occurring at the airport such as the increase in employment and sales of merchandise. Indirect impacts were estimated by looking at the expansion of industries and businesses which contribute directly to the airport's operation (e.g. hotels servicing airline pilots and stewards, aircraft maintenance, airline catering, etc.). Finally, induced impacts were estimated by assessing the effects of the 'chain reaction' as the cash injection resulting from the direct and indirect impacts stimulates the general economic activity. One can imagine the difficulties in quantifying these benefits, especially when attempting to make predictions several decades into the future. Once again, many of the same assumptions used to calculate an increase in passenger numbers in the SPASM simulation were also used here to estimate the economic benefits of airport expansion. Note that the predicted capacity requirement in the South East by 2030 was 300 million passengers per annum, i.e. SPASM assumptions included no options for redistributing capacity to other UK airports.

The original SERAS study did not include Gatwick airport. In 1979, the then state controlled British Airports Authority (now BAA PLC) came to an agreement with West Sussex County Council to *not* build another airport runway before 2019. Thus the original SERAS study omitted Gatwick on the grounds that the probability of expansion there was very low. This assumption was challenged by the county councils within which the Stansted and Cliffe expansion options are situated, and they took the DfT to court. In November 2002, the court judge made the ruling that options for expansion at Gatwick airport should not be excluded from the process.

Table 6  Economic benefits and costs of extra runways in £ billion with resulting passenger capacity

| Proposed extra runways with planned year of completion | Total South East capacity in 2030 (millions of passenger per annum) | Total benefits (£ billion) | Costs (£ billion) | Net benefits (£ billion) |
|---|---|---|---|---|
| Maximum use of existing runways | 202 | 6.7 | 1.8 | 4.9 |
| Gatwick (one close parallel – 2011)* | 217 | 8.6 | 2.8 | 5.9 |
| Gatwick (one close parallel – 2024)* | 217 | 8.2 | 2.3 | 5.9 |
| Heathrow (one – 2011) | 229 | 12.0 | 4.2 | 7.8 |
| Gatwick (one new wide-spaced – 2011)* | 238 | 11.1 | 4.1 | 7.0 |
| Gatwick (one new wide-spaced – 2024)* | 238 | 9.8 | 3.0 | 6.8 |
| Heathrow (one – 2011) & Gatwick (one – 2021) | 240 | 14.6 | 4.8 | 9.8 |
| Heathrow (one – 2011) & Gatwick (one – 2024) | 240 | 14.5 | 4.8 | 9.8 |
| Stansted (one – 2011) | 249 | 11.0 | 3.9 | 7.1 |
| Gatwick (one – 2011) & Stansted (one – 2021) | 261 | 13.7 | 3.9 | 9.8 |
| Stansted (one – 2011) & Gatwick (one – 2024) | 261 | 13.8 | 4.0 | 9.8 |
| Stansted (two – 2011 & 2021) | 269 | 14.1 | 4.6 | 9.5 |
| Gatwick (two – 2011 & 2021) | 270 | 16.1 | 4.5 | 11.6 |
| Gatwick (two – both 2024) | 270 | 14.2 | 3.6 | 10.7 |
| Heathrow (one – 2011) & Stansted (one – 2021) | 276 | 17.8 | 5.5 | 12.3 |
| Heathrow (one – 2011), Gatwick (one – 2018) & Stansted (one – 2024) | 291 | 21.0 | 6.1 | 15.0 |
| Heathrow (one – 2011), Stansted (one – 2018) & Gatwick (one – 2024) | 291 | 21.3 | 6.2 | 15.1 |
| Stansted (two – 2011 & 2018) & Gatwick (one – 2024) | 294 | 17.4 | 5.2 | 12.2 |
| Gatwick (two – 2011/2018) & Stansted (one – 2024) | 294 | 22.6 | 5.7 | 16.9 |
| Heathrow (one – 2011) & Gatwick (two – 2018/2024) | 296 | 25.3 | 6.9 | 18.3 |
| Heathrow (one – 2011) & Stansted (two – 2018/2024) | 296 | 20.9 | 6.2 | 14.7 |
| Heathrow (one – 2011) & Gatwick (two – both 2024) | 297 | 22.6 | 5.9 | 16.6 |
| Gatwick (one – 2011) & Stansted (two – 2018/2024) | 297 | 16.9 | 4.8 | 12.1 |
| Stansted (one – 2011) & Gatwick (two – both 2024) | 314 | 21.7 | 5.7 | 16.0 |
| Stansted (three – 2011/2018/2024) | 314 | 17.8 | 5.2 | 12.6 |
| Cliffe (4 runways – 2011/2021) | 315 | 17.3 | 8.8 | 8.5 |

* A parallel runway close to the existing runway at Gatwick would be significantly smaller than a new wide-spaced runway built further away.

(Source: SERAS Annex D)

### Activity 19  Comparing qualitative and quantitative assessment of impact

As a practical illustration of the non-quantifiable components of the SERAS analysis, I would like you to focus on two contrasting options. The first is Stansted, which already has one runway and, with its existing infrastructure, has the potential to handle up to 25 million passengers per year. Cliffe, on the other hand, is a totally new site with the need to construct everything – from runways to terminals to the supporting transport network – from scratch.

The DVD contains two OS maps, one of the Stansted region and one of the Cliffe region. You will be able to overlay onto these maps the planned runway developments including the land-take (one runway for Stansted; two runways at Cliffe by 2015 and a further two by 2030). The DVD also includes data on the impacts on the ecology, heritage, noise, water, air quality and employment. Compare the data on the two sites for development by 2015 (i.e. one new runway for Stansted and two new runways at Cliffe). Consider how important these various qualitatively-assessed impacts are to you, and provide a rating from low to medium to high impact for each of the two sites. (You may find this easier if you draw a table.) What criteria did you use to make these evaluations? What difficulties has this exercise presented to you?

Taking all the impacts in your table, and the relevant cost–benefit analysis and the envisaged total capacity by 2030 from Table 6, into account, which of these two sites would you choose for development?

## Regional consultation on airport expansion

In July 2002, the DfT issued seven consultation documents representing the UK regions depicted in Figure 14 detailing specific options for where and how airport growth might be accommodated, including the 28 options (24 South East plus 4 other regions) for airport expansion at 14 different locations within the UK. These options and locations were based on the South East and East of England Regional Air Service (SERAS) studies and the Regional Air Service (RAS) studies.

In these regional consultation documents, published collectively as 'The Future Development of Air Transport in the United Kingdom', the DfT made a strong case for airport expansion in the South East. It was stated that, for the South East, the expansion would result in £18 billion in direct quantifiable benefits, 80,000 new jobs and low air fares for everyone, while a constraint in development would mean that 'return flights from the main South East airports, if no new runways were built by 2030, could cost on average around £100 more than today'. The figure of £18 billion is linked to an estimated capacity for the South East of 300 million passengers per annum. Note that even at this stage the pressure was very much on to meet the full capacity requirements as estimated in the SPASM modelling, with limited consideration of the responses to the original national consultation.

Interested public and organisational stakeholders were invited to make their views known on the seven consultation documents, via text responses to questions contained within the documents, or via the tick boxes of a summary National Opinion Poll questionnaire (internet- and paper-based).

Overall there were just under 500,000 responses, although the bulk (437,000) came through organised campaigns and/or petitions, with the South East providing 300,000 responses. The overwhelming message from the consultation was of opposition to airport expansion on the grounds of noise, air pollution, road congestion, loss of land and impact on the environment, wildlife and local community, yet business interests made a strong case for expansion based on socio-economic grounds.

### Activity 20  Reading and listening to responses to the SERAS consultation

The audio programme, *Consultation within the White Paper*, includes an outline of the consultation process as described by Department for Transport personnel, interviews with a selection of stakeholders made during this consultation phase and a critique of the process. Readings 3 to 7 for Book 1 (details below) are the official responses to the SERAS consultation from five major organisations with an interest in airport expansion in the south east of England. (These readings are included in the Block 1 Readings booklet as well as on the DVD.)

Read through the readings and make brief notes in your learning journal on the different responses described. Then listen to *Consultation within the White Paper* and add to your notes by describing the other responses heard.

## Readings 3 to 7

**Reading 3**  Extracts from BAA's publication *Responsible growth*

BAA (British Airports Authority) owns and operates seven UK airports and also has stakes in several overseas airports. They are 'the world's leading airport company'.

**Reading 4**  *The future development of air transport* from SEEDA

The South East England Development Agency (SEEDA) is one of eight regional development agencies in the UK. They are 'responsible for the sustainable economic development and regeneration of the South East of England – the driving force of the UK's economy'.

**Reading 5**  *Proposed response to the Government's revised consultation on air transport in the UK* from Wandsworth Borough Council

Wandsworth Borough is in south west London and has a population of a little over a quarter of a million. It is one of 32 London boroughs. Wandsworth Borough Council is the local government body responsible for services within the borough.

**Reading 6**  *Stansted: the case against irresponsible growth* from Stop Stansted Expansion group of North West Essex and East Herts Preservation Association

Stop Stansted Expansion is a campaigning group opposed to the expansion of Stansted Airport. Their main objective is: 'To contain the development of Stansted Airport within tight limits that are truly sustainable and, in this way, to protect the quality of life of residents over wide areas of Essex, Hertfordshire and Suffolk, to preserve our heritage and to protect the natural environment.'

**Reading 7** *The future development of air transport in the UK* from the British Chambers of Commerce

Most UK towns and cities have a local Chamber of Commerce whose membership comprises local businessmen and women. They seek to represent the interests and support the competitiveness and growth of all businesses in their communities and regions. British Chambers of Commerce is the national collective of these groups. 'The British Chambers of Commerce comprise a national network of quality-accredited Chambers of Commerce, all uniquely positioned at the heart of every business community in the UK and representing more than 135,000 businesses of all sizes in all sectors of the economy – equivalent to five million jobs.'

### Study note

This activity entails reading five papers as well as listening to an audio programme and could take some time. The audio (approximately 30 minutes long) includes perspectives from five different respondents and there are a further four from the readings. If time is limited, you should focus on the audio and only pick out the sections that interest you from the readings.

You will go on to consider the idea of multiple perspectives in Book 2 so keep your notes in your learning journal. No author's response is provided for this activity.

## 5.4 The December 2003 Aviation White Paper

The various studies and consultations produced a mountain of information and opinion, which the DfT had to weave into a single strategy document for the future of UK's aviation over the next 30 years. The SERAS framework and other studies had little to say on how to balance the interests of various stakeholders from the national to the local and the environmental to the economic. Finding a balance between environmental and economic impacts, and various stakeholder groups, was left to the political process. A team of government ministers, headed by the Minister for Transport, Alistair Darling, had access to all the information and applied a range of weightings to the various studies and consultational responses. The minutes of the ministerial meetings, including the weightings applied, are still confidential in 2005.

The process outlined so far clearly shows that options had already been limited even before the government officials began drafting the White Paper. Decisions had already been made to accept unlimited passenger growth, and that the bulk of this growth should be accommodated within the south east of England. Thus the only major decision to be made at this stage was exactly where to site the expansion: Heathrow, Gatwick, Stansted or a new airport at Cliffe? Even here, it is difficult to identify a clear rationale for the final decision. The final decision contained within the Aviation White Paper was made behind closed doors by government ministers and their advisers.

These were the final recommendations:

> There is an urgent need for additional runway capacity in the South East.
>
> The first priority is to make best use of the existing runways, including the remaining capacity at Stansted and Luton.
>
> Provision should be made for two new runways in the South East by 2030.
>
> The first new runway should be at Stansted, to be delivered as soon as possible (around 2011 or 2012).
>
> The further development of Heathrow is supported, including a further new runway and additional terminal capacity to be delivered as soon as possible (within the 2015–2020 period) after the new runway at Stansted, but only if stringent environmental limits can be met. An urgent programme of work and consultation will be started to examine this issue further and to consider how best use can be made of the existing airport.
>
> In case the conditions attached to the construction of a third Heathrow runway cannot be met, and since there is a strong case on its own merits for a new wide-spaced runway at Gatwick after 2019, land should be safeguarded for this.
>
> In the Midlands, a new runway will be developed at Birmingham International Airport.
>
> No other proposals put forward during the consultation for new airports at alternative locations are supported.
>
> (DfT, 2003a, pp. 91,111)

In summary, the decision making was principally driven by data generated by the DfT reports (e.g. the 'Air Traffic Forecasts for the United Kingdom' and 'Valuing the External Costs of Aviation' reports) and regional studies (SERAS and the other RAS), and involved a series of national and regional consultations and direct lobbying by a range of stakeholders. The data and decisions made by DfT were contested (and supported) by a vast range of stakeholders during the consultation process, by directly lobbying the government and through the media. It is very difficult to identify the influence of these consultations and pressures on the decision-making process. For example, the final decision does not actually reflect the data proposed by the SERAS study – Heathrow was never considered for development in 2018, and thus there is no cost–benefit data available for this particular decision (see Table 6).

It is clear that at national level, the pro-expansion lobby got exactly what it wanted while some of the anti-expansion lobby attained minor victories at local level (e.g. no airport at Cliffe). Although potential impacts of airport development at Cliffe were estimated to be the lowest to the local population of all expansion options, development at Cliffe would have affected a nature reserve with a high density of bird species. It is interesting to note here that the Royal Society for the Protection of Birds is by far the most powerful environmental NGO in Europe, with a membership of well over one million, far outstripping any other national environmental NGO.

The Aviation White Paper sets a policy framework for airport development but it did not in itself authorise such development, as discussed in Box 5. Developments on the scale of airport expansion are subject to legislation such as Environmental Impact Assessment, which will be discussed in Book 2. In terms of legislation linked to the Aviation White Paper, a Regulatory Impact Assessment was carried out as part of the same process and was also published in December 2003. Subsequently, the Civil Aviation Bill, introduced to the House of Commons in June 2005, implemented some of the commitments of the 2003 White Paper. It set out to clarify and strengthen the measures available to deal with aircraft noise and the powers of airports to set charges reflecting local emissions of pollutants from aircraft.

## 5.5 Reaction to the Aviation White Paper

The immediate reaction by the aviation industry was highly favourable. It was clearly apparent that almost all of the demands of the aviation industry had been met. Andrew Cahn, British Airways director of government affairs, was quoted in the 17 December 2003 issue of *The Guardian* newspaper as saying 'I have to say we're pretty delighted'.

On the other hand the majority of the organisations representing environmental perspectives accused the government of abdicating its environmental responsibilities. The climate change targets for reduction in greenhouse gas emissions were not tackled at all while the procedures for payments of environmental impacts were left unclear. Who, for example, was going to get the 5p per passenger per flight for the noise impacts? How was the £20 levy on ticket prices going to cover the permanent climate change damage of greenhouse gas emissions?

### Activity 21 Critique of the White paper

Listen to the audio programme titled *Critique of the White Paper*. This includes the Department for Transport's account of the final decision and a critique from Peter Ainsworth MP and Richard Dyer of Friends of the Earth.

"AND OUR NEW CUPS ARE MADE OF ENVIRONMENTALLY-FRIENDLY MATERIALS, SIR!"

### SAQ 5 Reviewing the decision-making process of the Aviation White Paper

Drawing on the *Critique of the White Paper* programme and the rest of the case study material, review the decision-making process of the Aviation White Paper and the context within which it evolved. For this, you should use the factors first presented in Section 1.3:

1. Who were the decision makers? How did they arrive at their position of decision making? Which resources did they control? Which values underpinned their actions?
2. What was the decision situation? What was the context? What were the uncertainties? What actual and potential risks were involved?
3. What problems were posed by the decision makers? Which opportunities were apparent to them?
4. Which criteria did the decision makers adopt to structure the decision-making process?
5. Within which time-frame did the decision-making process occur, and what sequence did the various components take?
6. Who were the people affected by the decision? How was their participation in the decision-making process managed?
7. What kinds of decision support (theories, tools and techniques) were in evidence in the Aviation White Paper decision-making process?

## 5.6 The future

There are so many things going on after the date of writing this case study concerning aviation expansion that it would be futile for me to speculate on all the potential developments. The debate about aviation expansion and the recommendations of the White Paper has continued. Below I have focused on two key areas to watch.

### The European Union Carbon Emissions Trading Scheme

The mitigation of the greenhouse effects of aviation emissions will be a major issue of contention in the near future. The aviation industry is strongly resisting any introduction of taxation and/or regulation that would limit emissions. Any unilateral taxes are perceived to prejudice the aviation industry's competitiveness, so an EU and/or global approach is required. But the UK has been at the forefront of resisting aviation tax harmonisation across the EU. Instead, the UK government proposes an introduction of a global carbon trading mechanism as already prototyped by the Kyoto Protocol Signatories. An emissions trading scheme would require governments to set emissions quotas for each industrial sector. This would require industries which exceed their quotas to buy 'carbon credits' which would compensate for their excesses. The trading scheme would work on a supply and demand basis, where certain industrial sectors able to emit less carbon than their quota would be able to sell their credits. The price of the carbon credits would then depend on the supply from efficient or contracting industries and the demand from inefficient or expanding industries.

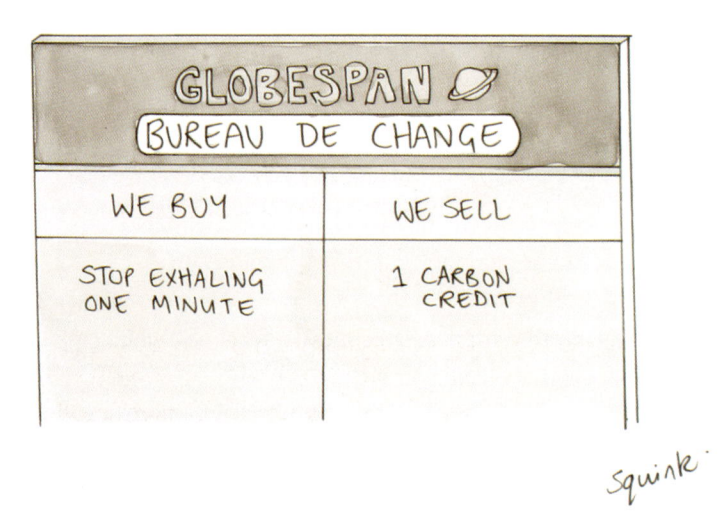

| GLOBESPAN |  |
|---|---|
| *BUREAU DE CHANGE* | |
| WE BUY | WE SELL |
| STOP EXHALING ONE MINUTE | 1 CARBON CREDIT |

*Squink*

The BAA has strongly favoured this approach, estimating that it would cost the aviation industry up to 40 times less than any potential taxes on fuels. The UK government is pushing for the inclusion of the aviation industry into a new European Union carbon emissions trading scheme to be relaunched in 2008. The European Union's goal of limiting global temperature rise to an average of 2 degrees centigrade is estimated by many scientists to centre around an atmospheric $CO_2$ concentration of 450ppm[*] (current levels are 380ppm). This provides an indication for the emission allowances that EU governments need to establish for various industries in order to not exceed the 450ppm ceiling.

[*] This is a unit for measuring gas concentrations for those gases found in relatively low concentrations in the atmosphere. Another way to represent $CO_2$ atmospheric concentrations is in percentage terms – 0.038%, i.e. 0.038 parts per hundred. Using parts per million (ppm) avoids using lots of zeroes.

"QUICK! STICK SOME MORE MONEY IN THE METER – THE EXHAUST'S CUT OUT!"

The jury is still out on whether carbon trading will effectively reduce emissions, or whether it will just provide a smokescreen for 'business as usual'. Many believe that the inclusion of the aviation industry in the scheme will create such a demand for credits that the price will reach astronomical levels and ruin the whole scheme. There are therefore many issues to resolve before 2008 and even European commissioners are favouring the introduction of aviation taxes as an interim measure. The UK government is resisting this.

## Runway capacity issues

There is still a long way to go before the bulldozers move into Stansted. Although the government has indicated that a new runway should be built at Stansted by 2012, it is now up to the BAA, the de facto owner of Stansted, to submit a plan for expansion for approval by the governmental planning authorities. This will inevitably involve a public inquiry, which will consult a range of local stakeholders and assess the impacts of expansion. A decision will then be made by a judge on whether a second runway should be built or not.

> **Box 7 The public inquiry process in the UK**
>
> Public inquiries are initiated by the UK government when significant reviews of the events are deemed necessary. Typical events that result in public inquiries are usually those that involve multiple deaths such as transport crashes or mass murders, but an important sub-set involve major infrastructural developments which now have a major public impact. Airport expansion falls within this category.
>
> A public inquiry is usually chaired by a well-known and well-respected member of UK society such as a judge, university professor or senior civil servant. These inquiries require the presentation in public of all evidence and the chair then submits a report containing recommendations to the UK government which usually approves the findings. This public submission of evidence significantly escalates costs. For example the Heathrow Terminal 5 inquiry involved the collection of 724 pieces of evidence from witnesses, 5900 documents, 27,500 written presentations and 100 site visits.

The BAA is currently trying very hard to improve its social and environmental image in order to help the plan receive a much more favourable response from the inquiry process. Stansted is just one of many airports across Europe where issues of runway capacity are being addressed. These issues are likely to be headline news for many years to come.

## Activity 22 Listening to Ugandan views on aviation expansion

Airport expansion within the UK will have global repercussions, not only as a result of contributions to climate change but also because the aeroplanes taking off from British airports will have to land somewhere. So expansion in the UK will almost inevitably lead to expansion in many airports throughout the world. The views of stakeholders outside the UK were not even considered. Take this opportunity to listen to the audio programme, *Perspectives from Uganda*, and consider: How does the situation in Uganda differ from that in the UK?

# Part Three

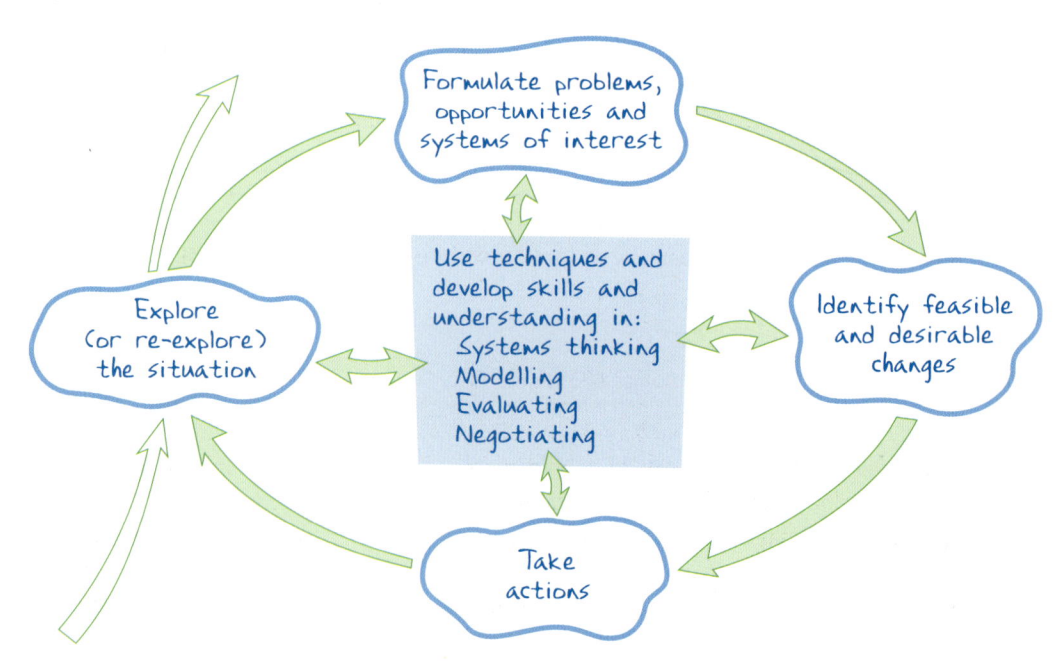

## 6 The T863 framework for environmental decision making

### 6.1 Environmental decision making as a learning process

This is the last section in this book. Perhaps now that you have read the 'Freedom to fly?' case study you will see why we have decided not to dwell too long on decision-making theory before turning to examples of what goes on in practice. There are many ways of making decisions, and there are different ways of describing decision-making processes and recognising their boundaries. I am now going to introduce one framework that the Course Team believes offers much to guide environmental decision making, and is a useful way of ordering our thinking about decision making. It is based on tried and tested ways of analysing decision situations and of working out appropriate courses of action. The overall purpose of the framework is to provide a structure to enable environmental decision making to be a process of learning that allows for continuous improvement rather than a one-off, constrained activity that stops once a decision is made. The framework we are suggesting is shown in Figure 16.

Figure 16    T863 framework for environmental decision making

## Activity 23 Engaging with the T863 framework

Go to the Resources section of the DVD and work through Part 1 of the material on the T863 framework for environmental decision making. This framework has a central place in this course, and it is essential that you engage with it.

(a) Have you encountered similar frameworks before? If so, make a note of your experience of using them (purpose, context, usefulness, etc.). If not, just note down your current understanding of the word 'framework'. (Record this in your journal or blog as you may find it useful later in the course.)

(b) What questions occur to you as you start to engage with this framework? (e.g. Is the language familiar to you? What do you notice about the arrows in the diagram? Is anything surprising or missing?) Note down these questions and observations now, as you will later need to comment on the framework, after you have used it, and your first impressions may be useful to you in commenting on your own learning.

### Study note

I have not provided my own response to this activity as I have been involved in developing the T863 framework so I cannot start to engage with it as if coming to it for the first time.

How does this framework compare with methods of decision making discussed earlier, for example the rational choice approach in Section 2.1? An important distinction between the framework shown in Figure 16 and other staged procedures for decision making is the iterative nature of the process described. Although in many cases a clear 'decision' can be identified, this may not be an end in itself. What may be more important is the opportunity that this process provides for those concerned to learn about the situation, and to be better prepared to deal with similar situations in the future. The framework thus represents a formalisation of the experiential learning process described in Section 4.3.

## 6.2 The T863 framework and the case study

Let us now use the framework to do a preliminary analysis of the environmental decision-making processes that are evident in the 'Freedom to fly?' case study and to consider what might be learnt from them for future use. Below I have listed a series of questions that may aid you in this analysis. As you work through this section and other parts of the course answering specific questions about the case study, you may sometimes feel you repeat some of the preceding activities. This is intended. Some of the activities reiterate or reformulate previous activities so that you build up both knowledge and skills – especially in a crucial component of Book 2, the re-exploration of environmental decision-making situations.

Does the framework help you to restructure your response to Activity 17 within the case study? Is it possible to map out the various stages in the Aviation White Paper process onto the framework? Can you identify areas where there is a mismatch between the process and the framework? Record your initial impressions of the framework and your answers to the following activity in your journal. My response is at the back.

> **Activity 24  Viewing the case study through stages in the T863 framework**
>
> Look at each stage of the framework in turn and, with the case study in mind, briefly answer the following questions:
>
> (a) How do you think this situation was explored?
>
> (b) How were the problem and opportunities formulated?
>
> (c) How were the boundaries established?
>
> (d) How were feasible and desirable changes identified?
>
> (e) What was the resulting action by the key decision maker, and how did the range of stakeholders react?
>
> (f) Do you think these stages were followed in a logical sequence?
>
> (g) Was there iteration between stages, and what learning do you think took place?
>
> (h) Which skills do you think were used by the decision makers during the process?

My purpose in asking the above questions is not only to allow you to make judgements about what should have been done with regard to the process of deciding aviation expansion with the benefit of hindsight, but also to point out that when similar decision-making processes are being started today, they could be approached differently. The advantages and disadvantages of different approaches will be discussed in detail in later course books.

In my experience, it is relatively easy to analyse a situation with hindsight, especially after having access to a range of pre-selected and ordered material. However, like many environmental decision-making situations, the Aviation White Paper was very complex and many constraints played on the decision makers during the process:

- time constraints may not have allowed a sequential procedure through the stages;
- the scale of the issue may have prevented all the stakeholders being involved in all the stages all the time;
- crucial information may not have been available at the start of the process and probably was revealed at different stages.

Like any framework, the T863 environmental decision-making framework has its potential strengths and its limitations, depending on how it is used. For example, in terms of strengths, it recognises the following needs:

- for problems, opportunities and systems of interest to emerge from exploring or re-exploring a situation;
- to use techniques and develop skills and understanding for environmental decision making in systems thinking, modelling, evaluating and negotiating;
- for environmental decision making to be considered as an iterative rather than a linear process.

The framework can also be used to help question and consider the decision-making processes in which you might be engaged. For example, it suggests questions such as: Has the situation been considered sufficiently? Have problems, opportunities and systems of interest been allowed to emerge? Will systems thinking, modelling, evaluating and negotiating help? Who has been involved in the processes of exploring a situation, formulating problems, opportunities and systems of interest, identifying changes and taking action and how have they been involved? What have we learnt from the overall process and how can that learning inform our future decisions and actions?

The framework's limitations (which it shares with other frameworks) are that it will not be possible to 'fit' every decision-making process to it, and that all steps in it will not be appropriate for all situations. You may also have time constraints in a particular situation that mean you cannot use all aspects of the framework. It will also not necessarily be easy to recognise where you are within it as, within one project or decision situation, several stages may be active at any one time. You should be as critical in your use of this framework as in your use of other aspects of this course.

Why the course team considers the above points as strengths and limitations will become clear as the course progresses. Once you have had a chance to use the framework yourself, you will also have your own view of its strengths and limitations in relation to how you have used it and the situations you have been considering.

Each stage of the T863 framework will be considered in much more depth and the 'Freedom to fly?' case study will be analysed in much greater detail, as you progress through the course books. In Book 2, you will consider how to explore or re-explore an environmental decision-making situation and how to formulate problems, opportunities and systems of interest. Book 3 will deal with identifying feasible and desirable changes, and will consider the consequences of recommending and/or undertaking action. Book 4 will provide you with the skills to critically appraise environmental decision making as a whole, including critically appraising the course framework and your role in environmental decision making. All the books will encourage you to use a series of techniques for environmental decision making and gradually increase your skills and understanding in systems thinking, modelling, evaluating and negotiating.

# Learning outcomes

## Knowledge and understanding

After you have worked through Book 1 you should be able to recognise and explain in your own words:

- some different approaches to decision making
- some major factors that influence decision making
- what you understand by environmental decision making and several key concepts that are relevant to it
- how to identify some environmental issues that are of interest or concern to you and explain why
- what the authors mean by a system, its boundary and environment
- that we each have a place in the environmental decision-making process in contexts ranging from individual to international
- that while each individual's effect may itself be small, it is still a contributing factor to the environmental decision-making process and outcome
- some of the principles of sustainable development that are relevant to decision making
- how environmental decision making takes place in the context of sustainable development
- the significance of values and power relations and sources in decision making
- some of the evolving discourse of relevance to environmental decision making and sustainable development
- some of your own perspectives, assumptions and motivations for engaging in environmental decision making
- the sequence of events that occurred in UK aviation expansion between 1998 and 2004
- the decision-making process that occurred during UK aviation expansion and the role of the UK Aviation White Paper process in decision making
- the stages of one generic process you may go through in attempting to reach a decision and take action (the T863 environmental decision-making framework)
- insights and conclusions from the analysis of examples of environmental decision making, including the case study.

## Skills

You should be able to:

- locate yourself in one or more positions in a hierarchy of environmental decision-making contexts when confronted with a particular situation
- use some relevant techniques for exploring concepts and issues – spray diagrams, critical reading, etc.

# References

Allen, T. and Thomas, A. (1992) *Poverty and Development in the 1990s*, Oxford/Milton Keynes, Oxford University Press/The Open University.

BBC News website (2005) www.news.bbc.co.uk/ (Accessed June 2005)

BBC Screenplay 2004 website (2004) http://www.bbc.co.uk/nottingham/culture/2004/01/screenplay_2004.shtml (Accessed June 2005).

BBC Weather Renewable Energy – Water web page (2005) http://www.bbc.co.uk/weather/features/energy_water.shtml (Accessed August 2005).

Blowers, A. and Glasbergen, P. (1995) *Environmental Policy in an International Context: Perspectives*, London, Arnold.

Boulding, K.R. (1996) 'The economics of the coming Spaceship Earth' in Jarrett, H. (ed.) *Environmental Quality in a Growing Economy*, Baltimore, Johns Hopkins University Press.

Brockbank, A. and McGill, I. (1998) 'What is learning? A review of learning theories' in *Facilitating Reflective Learning 1. Higher Education*, Society for Research into Higher Education and Open University Press.

Buckingham-Hatfield, S. and Percy, S. (1999) *Constructing Local Environmental Agendas: People, Places and Participation*, London, Routledge.

Chambers, R. (1993) *Challenging the Professions – Frontiers for Rural Development*, London, Intermediate Technology Publications.

Climate Care, www.climatecare.org/airtravelcalc/airtravelcalc.cfm, (Accessed August 2005).

Cohen, M.D., March, J.G. and Olsen, J.P. (1972) 'A garbage can model of organizational choice', *Administrative Science Quarterly*, vol. 17, no. 1, pp. 1–25.

Cooper, D.E. (1992) 'The idea of environment', in *The Environment in Question*, Cooper, D.E. and Palmer, J.A. (eds.), London, Routledge.

Development Gateway Business Environment web page (2005) http://www.topics.developmentgateway.org/businessenvironment (Accessed May 2005).

DETR (2000) 'Appraisal framework for airports in South East and East of England', Department of the Environment, Transport and The Regions.

DfT (1998) 'New Deal for Transport: Better for Everyone', Department for Transport.

DfT (2000a) 'Valuing the External Costs of Aviation', Department for Transport.

DfT (2000b) 'UK Air Freight Study – Part 1', Department for Transport.

DfT (2000c) 'A Study into the Potential Impact of Changes in Technology on the Development of Air Transport in the UK', Department for Transport.

DfT (2000d) 'Air Traffic Forecasts for the United Kingdom', Department for Transport.

DfT (2002a) 'The Future Development of Air Transport in the United Kingdom', Department for Transport.

DfT (2002b) 'Regional Air Services Coordination Study', *Rasco Final Report*, Department for Transport.

DfT (2003a) 'Aviation White Paper', Department for Transport.

DfT (2003b) 'UK Air Travel Forecasts up to 2030: Annex A to Aviation White Paper', Department for Transport.

DfT (2005), http://www.DfT.gov.uk, (Accessed January 2006).

Dryzek, J.S. (1997) *The Politics of the Earth: Environmental Discourses*, Oxford, Oxford University Press.

ENDS Report 366 (July 2005) *Environment under Pressure as EU Targets Jobs and Growth*, pp. 3–4.

English, M.R. (1999) in Sexton, K., Marcus, A.F., Easter, K.W. and Burkhardt, T.D. *Better Environmental Decisions: Strategies for Governments, Businesses and Communities*, Washington DC, Island Press.

Harcourt, W. (1994) *Feminist Perspectives on Sustainable Development*, London/New Jersey, Zed Books/Society for International Development.

Hardin, G. (1968) 'The tragedy of the commons', *Science*, vol. 162, pp. 1243–8.

Heron, J. (1989) *Facilitators' Handbook*, London, Kogan Page.

Holdgate, M. (1995) 'How can development be sustainable?', The Prince Philip Lecture, *RSA Journal*, November, pp. 15–29.

Holmes, P. (2001) 'Fly by numbers', *The Sentinel*, Stoke on Trent, 4 November.

Hopwood, B., Mellor, M. and O'Brien, G. (2005) 'Sustainable development: mapping different approaches', *Sustainable Development*, vol. 13, pp. 38–52.

ICAO (2000) Air Traffic forecast, ICAO, Geneva, available at http://www.icao.int (Accessed June 2005).

Johannesburg Declaration on Sustainable Development (2002) http://www.housing.gov.za/content/legislation_policies/johannesburg.htm (Accessed 6 January 2006).

Kates, R.W., Parris, T.M. and Leiserowitz, A.A. (2005) 'What is sustainable development? Goals, indicators, values and practice', *Environment*, vol. 47, no. 3, p. 11.

Klein, G. (1998) *Sources of Power: How People Make Decisions*, London, MIT Press.

Kleindorfer, P.R., Kunreuther, H.C. and Schoemaker, P.J.H. (1993) *Decision Sciences: An Integrated Perspective*, New York, Cambridge University Press.

Kolb, D.A. (1984) *Experiential learning: experience as the source of learning and development*, Englewood Cliffs, Prentice-Hall.

Kolb, D.A. and Fry, R. (1975) 'Toward an applied theory of experiential learning' in Cooper, C. (ed.) *Theories of Group Process*, London, John Wiley.

Macrory, R. (2005) 'Environmental assessment and outline planning application' in *ENDS Report 366*, July 2005, p. 55.

March, J. (1978) 'Bounded rationality, ambiguity and the engineering of choice', *Bell Journal of Economics*, vol. 9, pp. 587–608.

March, J. (1982) 'Theories of choice and making decisions', in Armson, R. and Paton, R. (eds) (1994) *Organizations: Cases, Issues and Concepts*, London, The Open University/Paul Chapman Press.

March, J.G. (1991) 'How decisions happen in organizations', *Human–Computer Interaction*, vol. 6, pp. 95–117.

March, J. (1994) *A Primer on Decision Making: How Decisions Happen*, Free Press, pp. 8–15, and reprinted in Billsberry, J. (ed.) (1996) *The Effective Manager*, London, Sage/Open University.

Orasanu, J. and Connolly, T. (1993) 'The reinvention of decision making' in Klein, G., Orasanu, J., Calderwood, R. and Zsambok, C.E (eds) *Decision Making in Action: Models and Methods*, Norwood, NJ, Ablex.

Quarrie, J. (ed.) (1992) Earth Summit, 1992, *The United Nations Conference on Environment and Development. Agenda 21*, London, Regency Press.

Schwarz, N. (2000) 'Emotion, cognition, and decision making', *Cognition and Emotion*, vol. 14, no. 4, pp. 433–440.

Sexton, K. and Murdoch, B.S. (eds) (1996) *Environmental Policy in Transition: Making the Right Choices*, University of Minnesota, Minneapolis, Center for Environmental and Health Policy.

Sexton, K., Marcus, A.F., Easter, K.W. and Burkhardt, T.D. (1999) *Better Environmental Decisions: Strategies for Governments, Businesses and Communities*, Washington DC, Island Press.

Simon, H.A. (1957) *Models of Man: Social and Rational Mathematical Essays on Rational Human Behaviour in a Social Setting*, New York, Wiley.

Thorpe, K. (1999) 'The Heathrow Terminal 5 Inquiry: an inquiry secretary's perspective', *Planning Inspectorate Journal*, Issue 15.

Ubel, P. (2005) 'Emotions, decisions, and the limits of rationality: symposium introduction', *Medical Decision Making*, vol. 25, no. 1, pp. 95-96.

UK Rivers Trust (2005), http://www.associationofriverstrusts.org.uk/ (Accessed January 2006).

UNEP DTIE website (2002) Division of Technology, Industry and Economics (DTIE) of the United Nations Environment Programme (UNEP) http://www.unep.fr/outreach/wssd/postjoburg/wssdoutcomes.htm (Accessed 6 January 2006).

United Nations Millennium Declaration (2000) Resolution 55/2, United Nations A/RES/55/2, 18 September.

United Nations Millennium Goals website (2006) http://www.un.org/millenniumgoals/ (Accessed 6 January 2006).

Uphoff, N. (1992) 'Local institutions and participation for sustainable development', *Gatekeeper Series No. SA31*, London, International Institute for Environment and Development.

US National Research Council (1999) *Our Common Journey: A Transition Toward Sustainability*, Washington DC, National Academy Press.

Vickers, G. (1980) 'Education in systems thinking', *Journal of Applied Systems Analysis*, vol. 7, pp. 3–10.

Webster, K. (1999) 'Hopes and fears for Local Agenda 21' in Buckingham-Hatfield, S. and Percy, S. (1999) *Constructing Local Environmental Agendas: People, Places and Participation*, London, Routledge.

World Commission on Environment and Development (1987) *Our Common Future*, Oxford, Oxford University Press.

# Responses to Activities

## Activity 1  Consider your own decision-making experience

(a) I used *rational* choice to help in deciding which applicant to appoint to the post of 'field assistant' on a project I was managing. Detailed criteria were developed for both person and post and all applicants were assessed against those criteria.

(b) *Rational up-to-a-point* decision making helped me decide which plants to grow in my garden this summer. Several plant varieties met all my criteria. There was uncertainty about weather conditions and my time and inclination for weeding; clarifying these uncertainties would have helped me further with rational choice but I did not bother to follow these up, so in the end my final selection was partly arbitrary.

(c) The decision for the complete removal of an old hedgerow on farmland opposite my house this spring as the birds were nesting seemed to me to be an example of *garbage-can* decision making. The hedge certainly needed attention at some stage as part of it was dead. However, uprooting the whole hedge rather than removing the dead sections, possibly at another time of year when it might have had a less damaging effect on birds, was due to the availability of a contractor's time and equipment, as a job elsewhere on the farm had been finished early. This factor was combined with the absence that afternoon of others both on and off the farm who would have made a different decision. (My 'conservation of birds' values are showing here. Someone more concerned with other aspects of the impact of the decision, such as the costs of equipment hire, would perhaps judge it differently!) The action of pulling up the hedge at that time resulted from the combined set of circumstances, not a 'hedge-centred' decision-making process!

(d) I subscribe to the view that 'You can tell whether it's the "right" decision by how you feel about it'. I decided recently that I could not go to a conference I was invited to attend – lack of both time and money meant that I felt the only rational decision was to decline the offer.

I then realised I was disappointed about the decision and that it did not seem the 'right' decision for me at that time, and that if I thought about it differently and considered it as an opportunity to progress several things I was working on, I could probably find a way to go. I eventually reversed my decision. This could be thought of as a second iteration in rational decision making, in that what I had done was to assess the decision against new criteria that had emerged, but in practice I reversed the decision because of how I felt about it, not because of rationality!

## Activity 3  Substituting words

(a) protection of natural resources and management of wastes
(b) effects of new developments such as dams, motorways, airports or factories on their surroundings

(c) set-up or context

(d) physical and biological elements

(e) context or 'space'.

In each case the word environment or environmental seemed to be used in a broad sense so I didn't find it easy to find substitutable words. However, there were different emphases and adjectives in each paragraph so I deduced that the words had different meanings, dependent on the context within which they were used. Considering these different paragraphs suggests to me that people use the term in different ways.

### Activity 4   Which issues are yours?

Issues that seem distant to me are gold mining in Peru and Azerbaijan's post-industrial hangover. Some that seem close are those about home building on greenfield sites, environmental awards for youngsters and opposition to wind farms.

Three examples of issues of interest or concern are:

(i) The idea of an award for 'greenest' roads. I am curious to know what is meant, and as a road and car user concerned about the impact of road building and use, I'm interested to hear more about what sounds like a move to limit detrimental effects.

(ii) Greenpeace's opposition to a windfarm plan also interests me because I lived for some time in Denmark where a lot of energy is generated by wind turbines and where there seems to be a lot less opposition to them. To me, windfarms provide a better alternative to power stations, which seem to have more damaging environmental effects (such as coal or nuclear). So I'm interested to know the nature of Greenpeace's objections.

(iii) The online campaign seeking a fishing ban also interests me. My perspectives are both as a consumer of fish and someone who enjoys seeing fish and other freshwater and marine life in their natural habitat in different parts of the world. I am also interested in the role of the Internet in environmental decision making.

### Activity 5   Engaging with multidimensional characteristics

(a) I have come across all the terms in the table before but I do wonder what the authors mean by words such as 'elite corps', 'deliberative', 'natural systems', 'persistence' and 'critical natural areas'. There is some qualification of these terms in the text of their book, so I have either looked these up there or made some assumptions about what is meant:

- Elite corps – seems to refer to senior members of responsible organisations. This mode of decision making is one where those who do not fall into that category do not participate in the decision process.

- Deliberative – organised for a process of deliberating or debating, which as it's in a category about urgency implies a longer time period is available than the 'urgent' category.

- Natural systems. I assume here that 'natural' as opposed to 'manufactured' is meant and that system refers to an assembly of interconnected components that does something. But I'm aware that 'natural' and 'made' distinctions often get blurred and 'system' is often used in a vaguer sense. The examples given regarding 'natural system scales' in the table are watersheds and airsheds, and while water and air are what I think of as 'natural', there is a lot about their use and management that isn't. I wasn't familiar with the term 'airshed ' (other than as sheds that house aircraft!) so I looked it up and found it to mean an area where common weather conditions behave in a coherent way with respect to air pollution in the atmosphere. As such it provides a unit for analysis or management in the way that a water catchment area does. My understanding of 'watershed' in this context is also what I would think of as a water catchment, i.e. an identifiable area rather than a boundary. My understanding is that terms such as watershed, water catchment and airshed are used in a range of different ways in different countries and traditions.
- Persistence – I presume this refers to elements that persist over a long time rather than break down, as with radioactive particles or some kinds of pesticides.
- Critical natural areas – I assume this refers to 'critical' in its 'crucial' rather than its 'finding fault' or 'evaluating' senses. But critical for what? Looking it up in their book, I note that Sexton et al. have given a definition as 'issues concerning the protection of areas such as coastlines, floodplains, wetlands, ecological bio-reserves, parks, and the habitats of endangered species'.

(b) A few examples of dimensions I have direct experience of:
- Levels – all the social levels;
- Domain – issues of critical natural areas and natural resource management: neighbourhoods (villages) and countries, watersheds; persistence (nuclear power issues) and context (my interest in 'trajectories' of decisions which incorporate past, present and future);
- Setting – individual acting as member of an organisation; environmental advocacy groups, community groups and affected or interested individual; urgent and deliberative decisions;
- Modes – emergency action, routine procedures and collaborative learning;
- Assumptions – I have come across all the assumptions about basic underlying causes of environmental problems (though I'm not entirely sure what's behind 'failure to use comprehensive approaches' so would need to check that one);
- Evaluation – I have also come across all the evaluation criteria.

From my own experience I would add 'multi-agency' as a social level of the environmental decision. I would add 'rural' to urban infrastructure/growth management from a UK context, and I would add 'ethical' to the criteria for evaluating environmental decisions.

### Activity 6   What does sustainable development mean?

(a) sustainable development; rational development; natural resources; welfare of people; economic advancement; market economic systems; sound growth; conserving our environment; quality of life; indefinable qualities; world; economic valuation; expediency; richness and beauty of nature; wonder of great landscapes; development process; test of success; stable world human population; diversity of plants and animal species; it can be done; won't be easy; adapting; costly; difficult; economic growth; development discourse; social, political, cultural, environmental and gender concerns; critiques of development; criticised and challenged; include environmental considerations; development professionals; poverty alleviation; mass poverty; environmental deterioration; gender bias of development thinking and practice; management of the environment; questioning the whole modernisation process and Western knowledge systems on which development is based; thinkers and activists have found their voices; political platform created UNCED; bring their concerns to the public arena.

(b) **My train of thought – economic?**

Economic advancement; market economic systems; economic valuation; costly; economic growth.

**My train of thought – what adjectives?**

Rational; sound; indefinable; world; economic; development; value; stable; costly; difficult; social, political, cultural, environmental; mass; whole; Western; public.

**My train of thought – how?**

Economic advancement; sound growth; expediency; value; it can be done; won't be easy; adapting; critiques of development; criticised and challenged; include environmental considerations; poverty alleviation; management of the environment; questioning the whole modernisation process and Western knowledge; bring their concerns to the public arena.

(c) One gap I noticed was that the perspectives of young people seem to be missing, although the Agenda 21 process and those that succeeded it did include 'youth' as a major group. There is also something about quoting from articulate people who have written their contributions, or had their words written down and reported, that makes me wonder whether there is a big gap in terms of the perspectives of the many people who do not communicate much in text, or who have never heard of the concept of sustainable development but still might make points for and against it if they had the chance. Perhaps some of the issues that might be of concern to them are here but how can I tell if I do not hear from them directly?

RESPONSES TO ACTIVITIES

## Activity 7  Raising questions about sustainable development

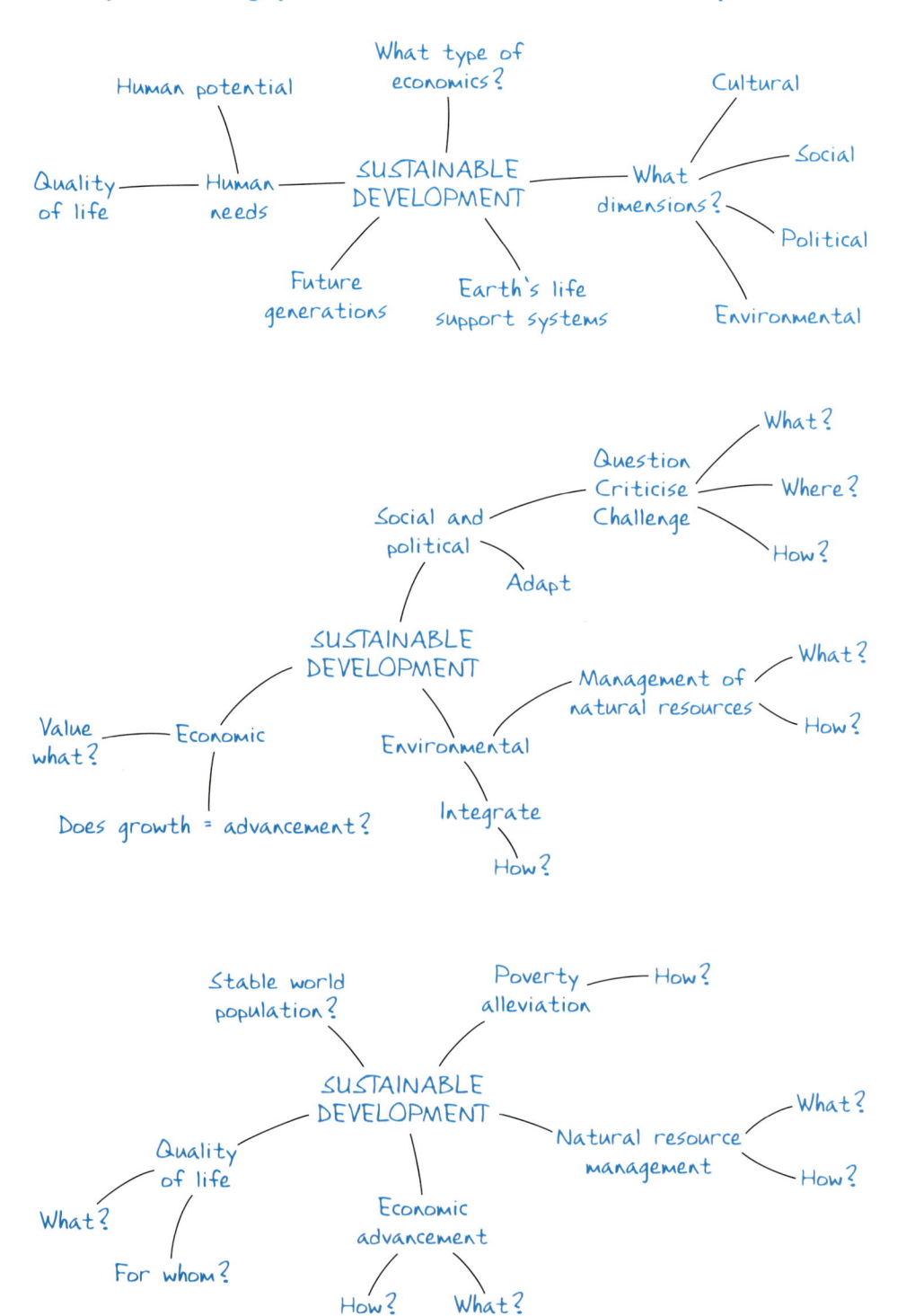

Figure 17  Spray diagrams in response to Activity 7

## Activity 8 Identifying your values

Three values of the kind suggested that are important to me are to do with nature, diversity and equality. While I find it fairly easy to identify these in a general sense, the detail of these values only becomes evident when I consider how I think and act in a particular situation.

In recent decision making, my valuing of 'nature' was a key factor in how I spent my time at the weekend, walking in the countryside. I am wondering about what I mean by 'nature'. (I am thinking of places where trees, flowers, birds and animals thrive and where I can see the sky and rural landscapes.) I also wonder if my example suggests a value that has more to do with 'experiencing nature' than actively doing something about enabling it to thrive!

## Activity 9 Recognising consistency in values

Many of the values underlying the Millennium Declaration are about people, and on the surface I find ideas of valuing democratic and participatory governance consistent with ideas of equal rights and opportunities of women and men, though it would presumably depend on how democracy and participatory governance were enacted. The 'respect for nature' value once again highlights an anthropocentric and instrumental view suggesting 'nature' primarily as a resource for people rather than having value in its own right. Ideas of shared responsibility among nations for managing worldwide economic and social development sound good to me, but given the prevalence of multinational corporations and regional as well as national levels (e.g. European Union) in decision making regarding economic and social development, I wonder what it means in practice. I will need to refer to the full document to find out what was intended.

## Activity 10 Sources of power

(a) I have chosen 'storytelling' from Klein's diagram.

I have been to many conferences as part of my job, sometimes as part of the audience and sometimes as a presenter. I have noticed that stories of people's experiences or events that they have experienced, if told in an engaging way, have sometimes stayed with me much longer than presentations in other forms. I have had feedback from people who have listened to my own presentations to indicate that others sometimes experience stories in a similar way. I have also listened to many presentations that have failed to engage my attention. I think it's tempting to think that a conference presenter is in a position of power and that their voice will be heard because they are presenting. But my experience is that it is only the presenter who has the ability to engage an audience who will be heard, and in turn be able to influence others, using storytelling as a source of power.

(b) I felt there was more to simulation than just 'mental' simulation and being able to imagine what might happen in decision-making situations I have experienced. I think I can see how that is a source of power at an individual level, but when working in groups, more explicit simulation or articulation of 'seeing the future' may be needed. Perhaps this would be done in modelling a series of possible shared scenarios, so it's not just about seeing the future but about modelling possible futures together with others? But perhaps I am also thinking of some rather different decision-making situations here from Klein, with less immediate time pressures?

I am thinking of a decision-making situation regarding moving house. My list of some of my sources of power for this decision-making process would be:

- imagining the future
- support of others in my household
- knowledge of my potential resources (e.g. money, time)
- knowledge of housing market and locations
- rational analysis of my options, circumstances and likely future circumstances
- intuition.

## Activity 11 Participating in environmental discourses

(a) I am familiar with most of the discourses that Dryzek has identified. Those in which I have actively participated most recently include discourses around environmental problems and sustainability.

(b) Examples of discourse in which I have participated include discourse on learning, in particular on social learning. Also on sustainable development. I see both as relevant to environmental decision making. Learning to use shared resources and deal with wastes with others or in a social context provides ways forward that complement other approaches such as regulation, legislation and market-led approaches. I see sustainable development as important context for environmental decision making.

## Activity 12 Your involvement in environmental decision making

The contexts of work, home, community and leisure are the main ones in which I make decisions that have effects on my environment.

One example of my environmental decision making as an individual is that I make purchasing decisions about consumables (food, drinks, household chemicals, etc.) and durables (clothes, furniture, electrical goods, etc.). This is environmental decision making because natural resources are used to make these goods, in their distribution and in some cases their use. Some of the resources used are non-renewable (although I cannot always tell to what degree because the labels on the goods do not give me enough details: for example, what energy is used to get them to me). Many of the goods are also wrapped in packaging which will become waste.

An example of my environmental decision making as part of a group is at work, where the T863 Course Team made a decision to use electronic conferencing instead of circulating papers, and in some cases in place of meetings. There were several reasons for this decision which included: speed of communications, suitability of conferencing for the tasks being undertaken (such as considering and contributing to ideas), making more effective use of meeting time, reducing use of paper and decreasing time spent photocopying. The decision was not, therefore, made primarily on environmental grounds but it had an environmental dimension, so I consider it environmental decision making. It would be simplistic to say that the environmental effects of our decision were all 'positive' effects in that some members of the group still choose to print out some of the messages, and it may mean that we use our computers for more time than we would otherwise. The decision to go for conferencing was a group decision but I still have choices I make individually about how I use the conference, and hence about the environmental effects of my actions.

### Activity 13    Exploring levels of environmental decision making

(a) My own levels of environmental decision making are individual, household and group level (as a committee member of a local charity), community level (with others from the group of houses at our end of the village), regional level (as a member of a local Nature Conservation Trust which draws its membership from several districts) and national level (as a member of a national environmental and development committee making policy decisions).

(b) I have worked on a couple of European environmental projects in the past few years, funded by the European Union, so I identify with a regional level that is between the international and national levels as well as the regional level between national and district level. This kind of regional level is not represented on Uphoff's diagram. As his work was trying to emphasise the local level, I assume he has just included that level within the grouping of 'international level'. It is indeed international but still identifies with a specific region.

(c) I can identify with the group and community levels easily enough. At group level, for example, I attend a local evening class where there is a certain amount of group decision making over use of materials, which is one environmental dimension. I am also on the committee of a local charity where we make many decisions about our use of resources, including transport and equipment. At community level, the people at our end of the village have collectively organised ourselves on occasion to take part in planning decisions. I cannot think of anything I am involved in at Uphoff's 'locality level' although I can think of an activity in which people from several communities are involved. I am a little unsure whether this would be a sub-district level activity, though, so I would need to read what Uphoff intended for each level to be sure. From my own direct experience I would only have identified two 'local' levels, so I have found Uphoff's diagram useful to make me think about other possible groupings.

(d) I have seen the area in which I live come under increasing pressure from road and housing development. I always feel I end up complaining after the event because I missed the opportunity to get involved at an earlier stage and to contribute more constructively. So I would like to be more involved at community and perhaps locality levels of decision making.

## Activity 14  How does aviation affect you?

In 2005, I flew from several London airports to Edinburgh, Scotland (for a conference), to Georgetown, Guyana (for research), and to Naples, Italy (for Christmas with my family). I wanted to calculate an approximate value of the carbon dioxide emissions resulting from my travels. To quantify this impact, I used an 'Air Travel Calculator' that I found on the Climate Care web site (**http://www.climatecare.org/airtravelcalc/airtravelcalc.cfm** – these web addresses can be short-lived, so if you are having difficulties accessing this site, then a search using the words 'carbon', 'emissions', 'air travel' and 'calculator' will provide you with a good range of alternative sites). I was surprised to discover that my three journeys have produced similar carbon dioxide emissions to a whole year of car use. In 2005, I drove approximately 16,000 kilometres which produced around three tonnes of carbon dioxide compared to the 2.5 tonnes emitted by my three air journeys.

In terms of constraints to flying, I am part of an extremely small proportion of the world's population that find it easier and cheaper to fly to the other side of Europe than to get public transport from my home to my place of work! I live within a 90 minute drive of all London airports and could readily find an offer to a European destination for less than £20 return, and I have no entry visa restrictions to any European country. Whereas it takes me six hours and £23 to get to work and back by train and bus (even though it is only a distance of 90 kilometres).

In fact, I live very close to Heathrow airport (a 15 minute car journey on a good day), so my family experiences the noise disruption and traffic congestion (with the associated air pollution) on a daily basis. On the other hand, at least four of my neighbours work at Heathrow airport so I appreciate the economic contribution to my local community, although I am worried about the increases in living costs (such as house rental) if Heathrow airport expands further.

Although I grow most of the vegetables we consume, I do occasionally buy produce such as tropical fruit and flowers, which I know have been flown in.

Beware that the figures provided here in my response to the activity are very rough approximations. There are some very significant implications in the online carbon emission calculations. For example, the calculations for air travel use only a single aircraft type with a standard number of passengers. The age and size of aircraft you fly in, and the number of passengers in your particular journey will significantly affect the actual emissions per passenger. So I would always recommend that you question the assumptions behind any modelling.

## Activity 15   Comparing two aviation videos

(a) To me, the *Reach for the Sky* documentary provides a very comprehensive coverage of social, temporal and spatial dimensions. It outlines the historical developments of aviation (post-World War 2) to the present day, the local and global impacts of aviation, and the wide range of social units involved. The last include the perspective of individuals, environmental non-governmental organisations, private businesses and local, regional and national government bodies, not only in the UK but from other countries in Europe and beyond.

(b) BAA's *Heathrow Terminal 5* video focuses, however, on the local social, economic and environmental aspects, with limited consideration of the regional, national and international context and impacts of such a development.

## Activity 16   Contextualising the Aviation White Paper timeline

I now find my own personal awareness of aviation-related events at the time of the Aviation White Paper timeline quite embarrassing. This was the period when 'no frills' carriers had first been introduced, so travelling by air had suddenly become more affordable. Between September 2000 and August 2001, I spent six months abroad working in three different continents (South America, Europe and Asia).

The aspect I now find troubling is that I never attempted at that time to connect my own personal travels with wider events both at policy level (i.e. the Aviation White Paper) and at other scales (as reported in the media). Even the impact of the terrorist attacks of 11 September 2001 barely affected my travelling. Writing this case study has made me reassess my flying habits.

## Activity 17   Considering questions that framed the process

My instinctive reaction to the challenge set by this activity is to propose a very different set of questions. I would want to first explore the role of aviation within the UK's transport situation (infrastructure, policy, attitudes, etc.) and look at how aviation complements and/or competes with both current and future potential developments in transport modes such as international high-speed rail. I would also want the process to address environmental impacts first and to implement sensible and practical compensation/remediation measures before delving into any major expansion plans. Finally, I would want to investigate radical alternatives to air travel including online conferencing and local tourism. Only then would I consider the three questions given.

# Activity 19  Comparing qualitative and quantitative assessment of impact

This activity asks for your own assessment of these impacts, so my response may well be different from yours.

|  | Stansted – one new runway | Cliffe – two runways |
|---|---|---|
| Noise | high impact | medium |
| Land/heritage | high | medium |
| Ecology | medium | high |
| Local air quality | medium | low |
| Water | high | high |
| Employment | medium | high |

The criteria I used differed for the various impacts. For noise and local air quality it was the total number of people affected; for land/heritage it was the number of historical buildings destroyed (I assumed residential buildings had low historical value); for ecology it was the rarity of the habitats (wetlands are critically endangered habitats); for water it was the scale of disruption; and for employment it was the number of people gaining employment.

The difficulty I found was the lack of information: for example, how was noise impact assessed? Personally, I would find evening noise significantly more annoying than at other times of day but the pattern through the day was not known.

From Table 6, the net benefit of Stansted (one runway) is £7.1 billion providing 249 million passengers per annum capacity. For Cliffe (four runways) the figures are £8.5 billion and 315 million passengers. (For Cliffe there is a difficulty in comparing the quantitative data with the qualitative assessment because official documents only provide data for four runways.) Taking all of this into account, I would choose Cliffe because of the lower impacts on noise, land and air quality combined with the better local employment opportunities and the greater passenger capacity. Having said that, I recognise I have a strong bias towards the human and social impacts rather than the ecological ones.

## Activity 22  Listening to Ugandan views on aviation expansion

In Uganda, the scale of the issue is quite different. Entebbe Airport is relatively small with far fewer flights per week than Heathrow, Gatwick, Stansted or other airports in the south east of England. Airport expansion in Uganda would be seen as a positive sign of development and a boost to the national economy. These social and economic concerns are more important than environmental issues. The constraints on airport expansion in Uganda are more to do with limited national resources than opposition by local inhabitants or any environmental concerns. There are some environmental impacts that are of concern but these are about wildlife and natural habitats rather than the impacts on human populations, which are the focus of opposition to UK airport expansion.

## Activity 24  Viewing the case study through stages in the T863 framework

(a) To me the exploration of the situation was severely limited. The focus was very much on forecasts of unrestricted passenger capacity. Consideration of other UK government policy, such as the 2003 Energy White Paper which demanded a cut in $CO_2$ emissions by 60% by 2050, was almost non-existent.

(b) The economy was a major theme analysed as a problem (if no airport expansion strategy was proposed) and an opportunity (increase in jobs and competitiveness resulting from expansion). The environment was not taken seriously so the 'opportunity' to resolve the environmental impact of aviation was not taken.

(c) The boundaries were very much framed through the choices made in the cost–benefit analyses of expansion options, and by limiting the transparency of the decision-making process. For example, the negative economic impacts to the UK economy of an increase in outgoing tourism were never considered.

(d) Feasible changes were identified mostly through the cost–benefit analyses, while desirable changes were identified through national and regional consultations.

(e) The limited exploration and the gradual closing down of options through the various stages meant that recommendations for significant expansion were inevitable. The pro-expansion lobby was 'delighted' by the decision while the anti-expansion lobby was left bitterly disappointed.

(f) There was a fairly logical sequence to the decision-making process although the identification of desirable changes through the various consultations seemed out of sync with the rest of the process, and in fact it is not at all clear how the consultations influenced the process or the final decision.

(g) No iteration occurred, with no review of decisions resulting from the new information (e.g. increase in oil prices) or stakeholder feedback. There is little evidence that learning took place.

(h) The skills used in the decision-making process focused mainly on the quantitative modelling (SPASM simulation, cost–benefit analysis). The use of systems thinking, evaluation and negotiation in the process was difficult to identify.

# Answers to Self-Assessment Questions

## SAQ 1 Information constraints

(a) problems of attention

(b) problems of memory

(c) problems of comprehension

(d) problems of communication

Organisations impinge on so many aspects of our lives it is sometimes difficult to tell when we are outside an organisational setting! But if, for example, I consider a decision at home where there are many options, such as 'How will I reduce my use of energy (electricity and gas)?', I seem to run into all four of the information constraints March refers to, just because I make a wide range of choices in this area. I have many electrical appliances (fridge, cooker, television, etc.), and both electric and gas heating, so deciding what and how to change, to reduce my overall use of energy, is a fairly complex task.

## SAQ 2 Concepts associated with sustainable development

The Brundtland definition incorporates the concepts of development, needs and intergenerational equity.

The US National Research Council definition includes concepts of nature (earth, biodiversity and ecosystems), life support (ecosystem services, resources and environment), community (cultures, groups and places), people (child survival, life expectancy, education, equity, equal opportunity), economy (wealth, productive sectors, consumption) and society (institutions, social capital, status, regions).

## SAQ 3 Environment and the Millennium Goals

Three bullet points are included under the 'environmental sustainability' goal. All three seem to assume anthropocentric definitions of 'environment'. The first is about integration of sustainable development into country policies and programmes with an emphasis on reversing loss of 'environmental resources'. It is not specific about which resources, but given the context of the goal I assume that it is linked to issues of livelihood. The second highlights 'sustainable access to safe drinking water' as a part of environmental sustainability and the third focuses on quality of life.

## SAQ 4 Mapping sustainable development

(a) The authors are referring to a shift in understanding relationships between humanity and nature and between people. They comment that this shift contrasts with the dominant outlook of the last two hundred years, especially in 'Northern' countries, that has separated environmental and socio-economic issues.

(b) They used the mapping methodology to help make sense of many different interpretations of sustainable development and to be able to compare them.

(c) The horizontal axis is labelled 'increasing environmental concerns' with three categories specified: virtually none, techno-centred and eco-centred (after O' Riordan's categorisations). The vertical axis is labelled 'increasing socio-economic well-being and equality concerns' ranging from inequality to equality.

(d) The three broad views of nature overlaid on the graph in Figure 1 are: (i) status quo, where a need for change is accepted but neither environment nor society are seen as facing problems that are impossible to overcome, so no fundamental changes are seen as needed; (ii) reform where there is acceptance of mounting problems, criticism of current policies but still no recognition of a need for fundamental change in society and in people's relationships with their environment; (iii) transformation where mounting problems are seen as rooted in society and in how humans interrelate and relate with their environment so transformation of society and/or human relations with the environment is needed to avoid a crisis or collapse.

(e) Limitations appear to be: The authors describe their framework as a broad conceptual framework rather than a precise mapping so exact locations of initiatives mapped are open to challenge. Classification into groups is a simplification and the location of boundaries and their nature are debatable. They recognise also that individuals and groups change their views over time.

(f) In the authors' view, the sustainable development discourse at present is dominated by the managerial outlook.

### SAQ 5 Reviewing the decision-making process of the Aviation White Paper

1 Alistair Darling was clearly the person with the final say in the Aviation White Paper. His mandate to govern as Minister for Transport was awarded to him by Tony Blair, the Prime Minister. The whole Aviation White Paper process was, in fact, underpinned by a series of decisions, such as the assumptions within the SPASM modelling, and yet the principal decision makers within the Department for Transport seem to have had a strong role in selecting outcomes which favoured airport expansion and significant resources were available.

2 The decision situation was certainly complex. Decision makers started in an environment where very little was known and studies needed to be initiated to provide quick results on predicted capacity and social, economic and environmental impacts. The decision makers had to balance local national interests and international obligations (chiefly as climate change), stakeholders from industry, the environmental movement and local residents, short-term gains and long-term impacts. The latter were highly uncertain, ranging from predicated capacity needs to socio-economic benefits to environmental effects. At risk were principally short-term political careers, competitiveness of UK aviation-related business and, in the long term, people's health.

3 The problems posed by the decision makers from the initial lack of an airport expansion strategy included loss of competitiveness of the UK aviation industry with capacity taken up in mainland Europe, and the risk of a protracted and costly public inquiry on submission of a development proposal. The opportunities included developing a clear strategy for expansion that supposed balanced social, economic and environmental impacts. I actually think that the decision makers

saw environmental impacts as a minor concern, with the notion of 'develop now, clean up later' (preferably by someone in the next generation) firmly in their minds. Resolving the environmental impact of aviation was therefore seen as an opportunity.

4   The rhetoric in the Aviation White Paper process was very much based around balancing socio-economic benefits and environmental impacts. One of the main criteria used was monetary valuation, i.e. that social, economic and environmental issues could be costed and compared so as to support decision making. Interested parties were consulted but there was no participation in determining the decision-making process, and indeed, the criteria which actually resulted in the final decision are unknown since deliberations were carried out behind closed doors.

5   The Aviation White Paper process occurred over the 2000–03 time period when major worldwide events were taking place which could have significantly affected the development, (the 11 September 2001 terrorist attacks, the Kyoto Protocol on climate change, preparation for war in Iraq, etc.). Yet the process did not seem to have adapted to the evolving worldwide situation.

6   The people involved can be divided into those under the direct influence of the decision – the travelling public, the aviation industry and related businesses, the residents surrounding airports, the environmental movement, and the various governing bodies (DfT, local councils, etc.) – those under indirect influence – the taxpayer (through subsidies to the aviation industry) – and those potentially affected by aviation's contribution to climate change.

7   Mathematical modelling to predict capacity requirements played a key role in the decision-making process. Cost–benefit analysis was also a significant technique used. Other techniques used included mapping, questionnaires and a wide range of environmental sampling techniques at the sites proposed for development.

# Acknowledgements

Grateful acknowledgement is made to the following sources:

## Text

Page 21: Sexton, K., Marcus, A.F., Easter, K.W. and Burkhardt, T.D. (1999), 'Characterising Environmental Decisions: Six Dimensions' in *Better Environmental Decisions: Strategies for Governments, Businesses and Communities*, Island Press.

Box 2: United Nations, 'The Millennium Development Goals'.

Box 3: United Nations General Assembly (2000) United Nations Millennium Declaration, **www.un.org/millennium/declaration/ares552e.pdf**

Page 38: Klein, G. (1998) 'How People Make Decisions', *Sources of Power*, MIT Press.

## Tables

Table 2: Sexton, K., Marcus, A.F., Easter, K.W. and Burkhardt, T.D. (1999), 'Characterising Environmental Decisions: Six Dimensions' in *Better Environmental Decisions: Strategies for Governments, Businesses and Communities*, Island Press.

Table 3: Dryzek, J. S. (1997), *The Politics of the Earth: Environmental Discourses*, Oxford University Press.

Table 6: DETR (2000) Appraisal Framework for Airports in South East and East of England, Department of the Environment, Transport and the Regions. Crown copyright material is reproduced under Class Licence Number C01W0000065 with the permission of the Controller of HMSO and the Queen's Printer for Scotland.

## Figures

Figure 1: Drawing by Vietor © 1982, *The New Yorker Magazine*, Inc.

Figure 3: © Photofusion.

Figure 4a: Carsten Peter/National Geographic Image Collection.

Figure 4b: © Reuters/NOAA.

Figure 5a: © Photofusion.

Figure 5b: © Ecoscene/Amanda Gazidis.

Figure 5c/d/e: © Photofusion.

Figure 6: U.S. National Research Council – Policy Division, 1999.

Figure 7: Klein, G. (1990) *How People Make Decisions*, MIT Press.

Figure 8: Harley Schwadron, Cartoon Stock.

Figure 10: Uphoff, N. (1992) 'Local Institutions and participation for sustainable development', *Gatekeeper Series No. SA31*, International Institute for Environment and Development

Figure 12: ICAO (2000) Air Traffic Forecast, ICAO, www.icao.int.